Early lives of Charlemagne - Primary Source Edition

Einhard, 770(ca.)-840, Notker, Balbulus, ca. 840-912, Grant, A. J. (Arthur James), 1862-1948

EARLY LIVES OF CHARLEMAGNE

Charlemagne

From a bronze statuette in the Musée Carn

EARLY LIVES OF CHARLEMAGNE BY EGINHARD & THE MONK OF ST GALL: TRANSLATED AND EDITED BY PROFESSOR A. J. GRANT

CHATTO & WINDUS : LONDON
MCMXXII

A LUI FINIT LA DISSOLUTION DE L'ANCIEN MONDE, À LUI COMMENCE L'ÉDIFICATION DU MONDE MODERNE.

LAVALLÉE

INTRODUCTION

The two "Lives" contrasted.—This volume contains two lives of Charles the Great, or Charlemagne (for both forms of the name will be used indifferently in this introduction); both written within a century after his death; both full of admiration for the hero of whom they treat; both written by ecclesiastics; but resembling one another in hardly any other particular. It is not merely the value which each in its different way possesses, but also the great contrast between them, that makes it seem useful to present them together in a single volume. Professor Bury remarked in his inaugural lecture at Cambridge: "It would be a most fruitful investigation to trace from the earliest ages the history of public opinion in regard to the meaning of falsehood and the obligation of veracity"; and these two lives would form an interesting text for the illustration of such a treatise. The restrained, positive, well-arranged narrative of Eginhard seems to belong to a different age from the garrulous, credulous, and hopelessly jumbled story of the Monk of Saint Gall. And yet the two narratives were divided from one another by no long interval of time. It is impossible to fix with any certainty the date of the composition of Eginhard's life, but there are various indications which make 820 a not impossible date. An incident mentioned by the Monk of Saint Gall makes the task of dating his work within limits an easier one. The work was suggested to him, he tells us, by Charles III. when he stayed for three days at the Monastery of Saint Gall, and it is possible to fix this event, with precision, to the year 883. We may think, therefore, of the Monk's narrative as being separated from that of Eginhard by more than sixty years, and by about seventy from the death of its hero. But in the ninth century the mist of legend and myth steamed up rapidly from the grave of a well-known figure ; there were few documents ready to the hand of a monk writing in the cloister of Saint Gall to assist him in writing an accurate narrative ; there was no publicity of publication and no critical public to detect the errors of his work ; above all, there was not in his own conscience the slightest possibility of reproach even if, with full consciousness of what he was doing, he changed the facts of history or interpolated the dreams of fancy, provided it were done in such a manner as "to point a moral or adorn a tale."

And so it is that, whereas through Eginhard's narrative we look at the life of the great Charles in a clear white light, through a medium which, despite a few inaccuracies, distorts the facts of history wonderfully little, when we take up the narrative of the Monk, on the other hand, we are at once among the clouds of dreamland; and only occasionally does the unsubstantial fabric fade, and allow us to get a glimpse of reality and actual occurrence. But now each of these narratives demands a somewhat more careful scrutiny.

Eginhard's Life of Charlemagne is a document of the first importance for the study of the epoch-making reign of his hero. Short as it is, we have often to confess that in the chronicles of the same period by other hands we can feel confidence only in such parts as are corroborated or supported by Eginhard. Its chief fault is that it is all too short—a fault which biographers rarely allow their readers to complain of. But when we consider how admirably fitted Eginhard was for the task which he undertook—by his close proximity to Charlemagne, by his intimate acquaintance with him, by his literary studies and sober and well-balanced mind; when we remember that he lived in a brief period of literary activity between two long stretches of darkness—it is tantalising to find him complaining of the multiplicity of books and restraining himself with a quotation from Cicero from writing at greater length.

The Career of Eginhard.—A sketch of Eginhard's career will show how well qualified he was to deal with his subject. He was born about 770, in the eastern half of the territories belonging to the great Charles, in a village situate on the lower course of the river Main. His father Eginhard and his mother Engilfrita were landowners of some importance, and endowed by will the monastery of Fulda with lands and gold. It was to this monastery that the young Eginhard was sent for education. The monastery of Fulda was founded under the influence of Boniface, the great Englishman, whose zeal had driven him from Crediton, in Devonshire, to co-operate with the early Frankish kings in the conversion and conquest of Germany. The monastic movement was strong and vigorous in the eighth century, and nowhere more so than in the eastern half of the Frankish dominions. Eginhard was trained under the Abbot Baugulfus, and showed himself so apt and promising a pupil that the Abbot recommended him for a post at the Court of Charles (? 791).

The imperial crown was still nearly ten years distant, but Charles was already the most glorious and powerful of European rulers. In spite of all his constant fighting and travelling his extraordinary energy found place for interest in calmer subjects, and he gathered round him in his Court at Aix the best of what the age had to show in culture, knowledge, and eloquence. In this circle the most striking figure was Alcuin of York ; but Eginhard soon made for himself a position of importance. Charles lived familiarly and genially with the scholars and writers of his palace, calling them by pet names and nicknames, and receiving the like in return. The King himself was David ; Alcuin, Flaccus ; Eginhard is called Bezaleel, after the man of whom we are told in Exodus, chapter xxxi., that he was "filled with the spirit of God, in wisdom, and in understanding, and in knowledge, and in all manner of workmanship, to devise cunning works, to work in gold, and in silver, and in brass, and in cutting of stones, and in carving of timber." As the allusion implies, Eginhard was no mere book-learned scholar, but had brought from his monastery school much technical and artistic knowledge. He has been called an architect, and many great buildings have been ascribed to him, but with more than doubtful probability. The minor arts were rather Eginhard's forte, though it seems impossible to define them. Contemporaries speak of his carefully-wrought works, of the many tasks in which he was useful to Charles, but without exact specification. A contemporary document speaks of him as supervising the palace works at Aix; or rather, one Ansegisus is described as "the executant of the royal works in the royal palace at Aix, under the direction of the Abbot Eginhard, a man possessed of every kind of learning."

He was of small stature, and this is often made good-humoured fun of by his fellow-scholars. He is called the dwarf, the midget, the mannikin. Theodulf describes him as running about with the activity of an ant, and his body is spoken of as a small house with a great tenant. He married Imma, a Frankish lady of good family. (It is merely a stupid legend that makes of her a daughter of Charlemagne.) He lived with her happily, and was inconsolable after her death. Before his wife's death and without putting her away from him, he had embraced the monastic life—a proceeding which in no way scandalised the ideas of that century. He was the abbot of many monasteries, which he held, in spite of the canonical prohibition, at the same time. Saint Peter of Ghent and Saint Wandrille, near Rouen, are those with which he is specially associated. He was on several occasions employed by Charles on important embassies, but was for the most part rather his secretary and confidant than his minister.

His great master died in 814, and Eginhard survived him for twenty-nine years, having lived long enough to see the mighty fabric of Charles's empire show signs of the rapid ruin that was soon to overtake it. He received from Lewis the Pious further ecclesiastical promotion, but still lived at the Court until 830. After that year his devotion to the Church mastered all other interests. He built a church at Mulinheim, and procured for it with great pains the relics of Saint Peter and Saint Marcellinus from Rome; and it was at Mulinheim, renamed Seligenstadt (the city of the saints), far from the intrigues of courts, that he passed most of the rest of his life. His wife Imma ("once my faithful wife, and later my dear sister and companion") died in 836, and Eginhard's deep sorrow at her loss finds pathetic expression in letters still extant. The political confusion and the utter failure of Charlemagne's plans must have increased Eginhard's distaste for public affairs. He died at

Seligenstadt (probably in 844). His epitaph gave as his two titles to fame his services to Charlemagne and his acquisition of the precious relics.

The Writings of Eginhard that have come down to us are—(1) the Life of Charlemagne ; (2) the Annals ; (3) Letters ; (4) the History of the Translation of the Relics of Saint Peter and Saint Marcellinus ; (5) a short poem on the martyrdom of these two saints. These writings are all, with the possible exception of the last mentioned, of high value and interest, but the Life of Charlemagne is by far the most celebrated and important.

The Life of Charlemagne is the most striking result of the Classical Renaissance so diligently fostered at the Court of Charlemagne by the Emperor himself. Its form is directly copied from the Lives of the Cæsars by Suetonius, and especially from the Life of Augustus in that series. Phrases are constantly borrowed, and in some cases whole sentences. This imitation of Suetonius has its good and its bad results. It necessarily removed Eginhard's work from the category of mediæval chronicles, with their garrulity, their reckless inventions, their humour, their desire to please, to amuse, and to glorify their hero, their order, or their monastery. Eginhard's Life is not without mistakes, some of which are pointed out in the notes; but it is an honest, direct record of facts, and for these characteristics we are, doubtless, largely indebted to Suetonius' influence. On the other hand, it was the example of his classical model that induced him to keep his work within such narrow limits. Compression was forced upon the Roman historian by the scope of his work, which embraced the lives of twelve emperors; and the life and reign of Augustus had already been fully handled by other historians. But Eginhard knew so much, and so little of equal value is written about his hero elsewhere, that his brevity is, for once, a quality hardly pardonable. Along with Asser's Alfred and Boccaccio's Dante it gives us an instance of a biographer who did not sufficiently magnify his office and his subject.

No other account of the Life and Reign of Charlemagne can find a place here. For some time English readers had reason to complain that there was no good and popular book dealing with the great Charles, for Gibbon's chapter is admittedly not among the best parts of his history. But of late this reproach has been taken away. The two concluding volumes of Dr Hodgkin's great work, entitled "Italy and her Invaders," deal with Charles and his relations with Italy (vols. vii. and viii. "The Frankish Invasions" and "The Frankish Empire"). Dr Hodgkin has also written a general sketch of the whole of Charles's career ("Charles the Great." Foreign Statesmen Series. Macmillan). More recently, Mr Carless Davis has written a "Life of Charlemagne" for the Heroes of the Nations Series.

It is in works such as these (to mention no others) and not in Eginhard that the real historical significance of Charlemagne's life-work appears. Eginhard stood too near to his hero, and had too little sense of historical perspective to realise the abiding greatness of what Charles accomplished. It is the lapse of 1100 years that has brought into increasing clearness the importance of those years which lie like a great watershed between the ancient and the mediæval world. Of him, as of most great rulers, it is true that he "builded better than he knew." His empire soon became a tradition, his intellectual revival was eclipsed by a further plunge into the "Dark Ages," but all that he did was not swept away. With him ends the ruin of the ancient world, and with him begins the building up of the mediæval and modern world.

He did not find in Eginhard an entirely worthy biographer; but the "mannikin's" work has received unstinted praise since the time when it was written.

It was praised by a contemporary as recalling the elegance of the classical authors; its popularity during the Middle Ages is attested to by the existence of sixty manuscript copies; and a French editor has declared that we have to go on to the thirteenth century, and to Joinville's Life of St Louis, before we find a rival in importance to Eginhard's Life of Charlemagne.

The Monk of Saint Gall, it seems, must remain anonymous, for the attempt to identify him with Notker rests on no better foundation than the fact, or supposition, that both stammered. And this seems to be supposition rather than fact. We are, indeed, told on good authority that Notker stammered; but the view that the Monk of Saint Gall suffered from the same defect rests only on a sentence in Chapter XVII., where he contrasts the swift, direct glance of others with his own slow and rambling narrative—"Which I have been trying to unfold, though a stammerer, and toothless" ("quæ ego *balbus et edentalus* explicare tentavi"). It seems impossible to think that the words here must be taken in their literal sense. As the author is writing, not speaking, any defect of voice or teeth would in no way hinder his narrative: it is clear that the words are a piece of conventional and metaphorical depreciation.

We know, then, nothing of the author beyond what he tells us in his narrative ; and he tells us little, except that he was a German, and a monk in the Monastery of Saint Gall when Grimald and Hartmuth were abbots ; that he had never himself been in Western Frankland, but had seen the Emperor Charles III. during his three days' stay in the monastery, and at his bidding had written an account of Charles the Great, and his deeds and ways.

The monastery in which he wrote has a special interest for our islands ; for Saint Gall was an Irishman of noble family, and an inmate of a monastery in County Down, which was at that time governed by Saint Comgel. He was one of the twelve monks who in 585 followed Saint Columban into Frankland. Switzerland was the great scene of his evangelical labours. The Catholic Church celebrates his death on the 16th October ; and tells in the *Lectiones* of that day how he destroyed the idols of the heathen ; how he turned many to Christianity, and, even to the monastic life ; how he founded the Monastery of Saint Gall in his eighty-fifth year, and died at the age of ninety-five, having previously been warned in a dream of the death of his master, Saint Columban ; and how at once miracles declared that a saint had passed away. His monastery for a century followed the rule of Saint Columban, and then, in common with most monastic institutions of Western Europe, adopted the rule of Saint Benedict.

It was in the famous abbey, that owed its foundation to this Irish missionary, that this account of the deeds of Charlemagne—the Gesta Karoli—was written. The author is at more pains than we should expect to tell us from what sources he derived his information. The preface to the work is lost; but at the end of the first book he repeats some of the information that he had inserted in it. It was his intention, he informs us, to follow three authorities, and three authorities only; but of these three he seems to mention two only—Werinbert, a monk of Saint Gall, who died just as he was completing the first part; and Adalbert, the father of Werinbert, who followed Kerold, the brother of Queen Hildigard, in the wars that were fought, under Charlemagne's banner, against the Huns and the Saxons and Slavs. It is an amusing picture that he gives us, at the end of the first book, of Adalbert's anxiety to tell him of Charles's exploits and his own unwillingness to hear. It is to be presumed that the stories were often repeated, for not only facts but words seem to have remained in the mind of the unwilling listener. The third authority does not seem to be mentioned, unless he means to imply that Kerold himself (who was killed in an expedition against the Avars in 799) is one of his sources of information.

The whole of what the Monk of Saint Gall wrote is not left to us. The preface, as we have seen, is missing, and also, perhaps, a third book; for in the sixteenth chapter of the second book it seems that our author promises us an account of the habits of Charles, his *cotidiana conversatio*, when the story of his military exploits has been finished. But this may easily be a misunderstanding of his meaning; or, rather, it may be giving too great a precision to it. The good Monk is so little able to follow out any line of thought, or to maintain any arrangement, that it may well be that the "daily conversation" of Charles never received any separate treatment.

No attempt will be made here to estimate the historical value of the narrative, though it would be a matter of curious speculation to consider whether the critical historian can employ any method whereby a residuum of objective fact can be separated from the mass of legend, saga, invention, and reckless blundering of which the greater part of the book is made up. But, apart from any value which it may possess as a historical document, the Monk's story is of great interest for the light which it throws on the methods and outlook of a monk of the early Middle Ages. Charles has been dead not much more than half-a-century; the author has talked familiarly with those who knew him and fought under him; and yet the Charlemagne legend has already begun. Charles is already, if not inspired, at least supernaturally wise; if he does not work miracles, miracles are wrought in his presence, and on his behalf; if he does not yet lead the armies of Christendom to Jerusalem, he is already the specially recognised protector of the Holy City. There are passages too, as, for instance, the account of the visit of the envoys of the Greek Emperor, and Charles's "iron-march to Pavia," where we seem to detect the existence of a popular saga—a poem—underlying the prose narrative. With the help of M. Gaston Paris's "*Histoire Poétique de Charlemagne*," we can trace the further development of the legend. By the eleventh century Charles was already a martyr for the faith, and the Crusaders believed themselves to be passing along his route to Jerusalem. "Turpin's" chronicle, in the eleventh century, shows the vast extension of the legend, which now loses all but the vaguest relation to the actual events of history and the real characteristics of Charles. In the twelfth century (1165) Charles was solemnly canonised; and thenceforward the story spread into all lands, and received its last stroke in the time of the Renaissance, at the hands of Pulci, Boiardo, and Ariosto. These poets chiefly concern themselves, however, with the paladins of Charles; and the King himself forms the dimly-conceived centre, round whom the whole story revolves, deciding disputes, besieging the Turks in Paris, priest-like rather than royal in his main features, and by Ariosto treated with some irony and banter. These mediæval legends of Charlemagne may well be compared to those which deal with Virgil, whose transformation into a magician is not less remarkable than Charles's development into a saint. If the Charlemagne legend ends with Ariosto, Dante may be said to have given the last shape to the many transformations of Virgil, when, more than two centuries before Ariosto's "Orlando," Virgil acted as guide to Dante through the "lost folk" of the Inferno, and the toilsome ascent of Purgatory, until he handed him over at last into the keeping of Beatrice at the gate of the earthly Paradise.

Story and myth naturally attach themselves only to the greatest figures; and the Monk of Saint Gall's narrative becomes then, even by virtue of its inventions and unrealities, a testimony to the effect produced on the mind of his century by the career of Charles.

Both the life of Eginhard and the Monk's narrative have been translated from Jaffé's "Bibliotheca Rerum Germanicarum"; which, both in its reading and arrangement, differs at times considerably from the text given in Pertz's "Monumenta Germaniæ Historica."

CONTENTS

THE LIFE OF CHARLE-MAGNE BY EGINHARD

THE PROLOGUE OF WALAFRID

THE following account of that most glorious Emperor Charles was written, as is well known, by Eginhard, who amongst all the palace officials of that time had the highest praise not only for learning but also for his generally high character; and, as he was himself present at nearly all the events that he describes, his account has the further advantage of the strictest accuracy.

He was born in eastern Frankland, in the district that is called Moingewi, and it was in the monastery of Fulda, in the school of Saint Boniface the Martyr, that his boyhood received its first training. Thence he was sent by Baugolf, the abbot of the monastery, to the palace of Charles, rather on account of his remarkable talents and intelligence, which even then gave bright promise of his wisdom that was to be so famous in later days, than because of any advantage of birth. Now, Charles was beyond all kings most eager in making search for wise men and in giving them such entertainment that they might pursue philosophy in all comfort. Whereby, with the help of God, he rendered his kingdom, which, when God committed it to him, was dark and almost wholly blind (if I may use such an expression), radiant with the blaze of fresh learning, hitherto unknown to our barbarism. But now once more men's interests are turning in an opposite direction, and the light of wisdom is less loved, and in most men is dying out.

And so this little man—for he was mean of stature —gained so much glory at the Court of the wisdom-loving Charles by reason of his knowledge and high character that among all the ministers of his royal Majesty there was scarce anyone at that time with whom that most powerful and wise King discussed his private affairs more willingly. And, indeed, he deserved such favour, for not only in the time of Charles, but even more remarkably in the reign of the Emperor Lewis, when the commonwealth of the Franks was shaken with many and various troubles, and in some parts was falling into ruin, he so wonderfully and providentially balanced his conduct, and, with the protection of God, kept such a watch over himself, that his reputation for cleverness, which many had envied and many had mocked at, did not untimely desert him nor plunge him into irremediable dangers.

This I have said that all men may read his words without doubting, and may know that, while he has given great glory to his great leader, he has also provided the curious reader with the most unsullied truth.

I, Strabo, have inserted the headings and the decorations as seemed well to my own judgement that he who seeks for any point may the more easily find what he desires.

Here ends the Prologue

THE LIFE OF THE EMPEROR CHARLES

WRITTEN BY EGINHARD

HAVING made up my mind to write an account of the life and conversation, and to a large extent of the actions of my lord and patron King Charles, of great and deservedly glorious memory, I have compressed my task within the narrowest possible limits. My aim has been on the one hand to insert everything of which I have been able to find an account; and on the other to avoid offending the fastidious by telling each new incident at wearisome length. Above all, I have tried to avoid offending in this new book those who look down upon even the monuments of antiquity written by learned and eloquent men.

There are, I do not doubt, many men of learning and leisure who feel that the life of the present day must not be utterly neglected, and that the doings of our own time should not be devoted to silence and forgetfulness as wholly unworthy of record; who, therefore, have such love of fame that they would rather chronicle the great deeds of others in writings, however poor, than, by abstaining from writing, allow their name and reputation to perish from the memory of mankind. But, even so, I have felt that I ought not to hold my hand from the composition of this book, for I knew that no one could write of these events more truthfully than I could, since I was myself an actor in them, and, being present, knew them from the testimony of my own eyes; while I could not certainly know whether anyone else would write them or no. I thought it better, therefore, to join with others in committing this story to writing for the benefit of posterity rather than to allow the shades of oblivion to blot out the life of this King, the noblest and greatest of his age, and his famous deeds, which the men of later times will scarcely be able to imitate.

Another reason, and not, I think, a foolish one, occurred to me, which even by itself would have been strong enough to persuade me to write—the care, I mean, that was taken with my upbringing, and the unbroken friendship which I enjoyed with the King himself and his children from the time when first I began to live at his Court. For in this way he has so bound me to himself, and has made me his debtor both in life and death, that I should most justly be considered and condemned as ungrateful if I were to forget all the benefits that he conferred upon me and were to pass over in silence the great and glorious deeds of a man who was so kind to me; if I were to allow his life to remain as unchronicled and unpraised, as if he had never lived, when that life deserves not merely the efforts of my poor talents, which are insignificant, small and almost non-existent, but all the eloquence of a Cicero.

So here you have a book containing the life of that great and glorious man. There is nothing for you to wonder at or admire except his deeds; unless, indeed, it be that I, a barbarian, and little versed in the Roman tongue, have imagined that I could write Latin inoffensively and usefully, and have become so swollen with impudence as to despise Cicero's words when, speaking about Latin writers in the first book of the Tusculans, he says: "If a man commits his thoughts to paper when he can neither arrange them well nor write them agreeably, nor furnish pleasure of any kind to the reader, he is recklessly misusing both his leisure and his paper." The great orator's opinion would, perhaps, have deterred me from writing if I had not fortified myself with the reflection that I ought to risk the condemnation of men, and bring my poor talents into peril by writing, rather than spare my reputation and neglect this great man's memory.

The Preface ends: the Book begins

THE race of the Merovings from which the Franks were accustomed to choose their kings is reckoned as lasting to King Hilderich, who, by the order of Stephen, the Roman Pontiff, was deposed, tonsured, and sent into a monastery. But this race, though it may be regarded as finishing with him, had long since lost all power, and no longer possessed anything of importance except the empty royal title. For the wealth and power of the kingdom was in the hands of the Præfects of the Court, who were called Mayors of the Palace, and exercised entire sovereignty. The King, contented with the mere royal title, with long hair and flowing beard, used to sit upon the throne and act the part of a ruler, listening to ambassadors, whencesoever they came, and giving them at their departure, as though of his own power, answers which he had been instructed or commanded to give. But this was the only function that he performed, for besides the empty royal title and the precarious life income which the Præfect of the Court allowed him at his pleasure he had nothing of his own except one estate with a very small revenue, on which he had his house, and from which he drew the few servants who performed such services as were necessary and made him a show of deference. Where-ever he had to go he travelled in a waggon, drawn in rustic style by a pair of oxen, and driven by a cowherd. In this fashion he used to go to the palace and to the general meetings of the people, which were held yearly for the affairs of the kingdom; in this fashion he returned home. But the Præfect of the Court looked after the administration of the kingdom and all that had to be done or arranged at home or abroad.

2. When Hilderich was deposed Pippin, the father of King Charles, was performing the duties of Mayor of the Palace as if by hereditary right. For his father Charles, who put down the tyrants who were claiming dominion for themselves through all Frankland, and so crushed the Saracens, when they were attempting to conquer Gaul, in two great battles (the one in Aquitania, near the city of Poitiers, the other near Narbonne, on the river Birra), that he forced them to return into Spain—his father Charles had nobly administered the same office, and had inherited it from

his father Pippin. For the people did not usually give this honour except to such as were distinguished for the renown of their family and the extent of their wealth.

This office, then, was handed down from his father and his grandfather to Pippin, the father of King Charles, and to his brother Carloman. He exercised it for some years conjointly with his brother Carloman on terms of the greatest harmony, still in nominal subordination to the above-mentioned King Hilderich. But then his brother Carloman, for some unknown cause, but probably fired with love of the contemplative life, abandoned the toilsome administration of a temporal kingdom and retired to Rome in search of peace. There he changed his dress, and, becoming a monk in the monastery upon Mount Soracte, built near the church of the blessed Silvester, enjoyed for some years the quiet that he desired, with many brethren, who joined themselves to him for the same purpose. But as many of the nobles of Frankland came on pilgrimage to Rome to perform their vows, and, unwilling to pass by one who had once been their lord, interrupted the peace that he most desired by frequent visits, he was compelled to change his abode. For, seeing that the number of his visitors interfered with his purpose, he left Mount Soracte and retired to the monastery of Saint Benedict, situated in the camp of Mount Cassino, in the province of Samnium. There he occupied what remained to him of this temporal life in religious exercises.

3. But Pippin, after he was made King instead of Mayor of the Palace by the authority of the Roman Pontiff, exercised sole rule over the Franks for fifteen years, or rather more. Then, after finishing the Aquitanian war, which he had undertaken against Waifar, Duke of Aquitania, and had carried on for nine consecutive years, he died at Paris of the dropsy, and left behind him two sons, Charles and Carloman, to whom by divine will the succession of the kingdom came. For the Franks called a solemn public assembly, and elected both of them to be kings, on the understanding that they should equally divide the whole kingdom, but that Charles should receive for his special administration that part which his father Pippin had held, while Carloman received the territories ruled by their uncle Carloman. The conditions were accepted, and each received the share of the kingdom that was allotted to him. Harmony was maintained between the two brothers, though not without difficulty; for many partisans of Carloman tried to break their alliance, and some even hoped to engage them in war. But the course of events proved

that the danger to Charles was imaginary rather than real. For, upon the death of Carloman, his wife with her sons and some of the leading nobles fled to Italy, and, for no obvious reason, passed over her husband's brother, and placed herself and her children under the protection of Desiderius, King of the Lombards. Carloman, after ruling the kingdom for two years conjointly with Charles, died of disease, and Charles, upon the death of Carloman, was made sole king with the consent of all the Franks.

4. It would be foolish of me to say anything about his birth and infancy, or even about his boyhood, for I can find nothing about these matters in writing, nor does anyone survive who claims to have personal knowledge of them. I have decided, therefore, to pass on to describe and illustrate his acts and his habits and the other divisions of his life without lingering over the unknown. I shall describe first his exploits both at home and abroad, then his habits and interests, and lastly the administration of the kingdom and the end of his reign, omitting nothing that demands or deserves to be recorded.

PART I

HIS EXPLOITS AT HOME AND ABROAD

5. Of all the wars that he waged that in Aquitania, begun, but not finished, by his father, was the first that he undertook, because it seemed easy of accomplishment. His brother was still alive, and was called upon for assistance, and, though he failed to provide the help that he promised, Charles prosecuted the enterprise that he had undertaken with the utmost energy, and would not desist or slacken in his task before, by perseverance and continuous effort, he had completely reached the end after which he strove. For he forced Hunold, who after the death of Waifar had attempted to occupy Aquitania and renew the almost finished war, to abandon Aquitania and retire into Gascony. Even there he did not allow him to remain, but crossed the Garonne, and sent ambassadors to Lupus, Duke of the Gascons, ordering him to surrender the fugitive,

and threatening him with war unless he did so at once. Lupus, more wisely, not only surrendered Hunold but also submitted himself and the province over which he presided to the power of Charles.

6. When the Aquitanian trouble was settled and the war finished, when, too, his partner in the kingdom had withdrawn from the world's affairs, he undertook a war against the Lombards, being moved thereto by the entreaties and the prayers of Hadrian, Bishop of the City of Rome. Now, this war, too, had been undertaken by his father at the supplication of Pope Stephen, under circumstances of great difficulty, inasmuch as certain of the chiefs of the Franks, whose advice he was accustomed to ask, so strongly resisted his wishes that they openly declared that they would leave their King to return home. But now Charles undertook the war against King Haistulf, and most swiftly brought it to an end. For, though his reasons for undertaking the war were similar to, and, indeed, the same as those of his father, he plainly fought it out with a very different energy, and brought it to a different end. For Pippin, after a siege of a few days at Pavia, forced King Haistulf to give hostages, and restore to the Romans the towns and fortresses that he had taken from

them, and to give a solemn promise that he would not attempt to regain what he had surrendered. But King Charles, when once he had begun the war, did not stop until he had received the surrender of King Desiderius, whom he had worn down after a long siege; until he had forced his son Adalgis, in whom the hopes of his people seemed to be centred, to fly not only from his kingdom but from Italy; until he had restored to the Romans all that had been taken from them; until he had crushed Hruodgausus, Præfect of the Duchy of Friuli, who was attempting a revolution; until, in fine, he had brought all Italy under his rule, and placed his son Pippin as king over the conquered country. I should describe here the difficulties of the passage of the Alps and the vast toil with which the Franks found their way through the pathless mountain ridges, the rocks that soared to heaven, and the sharply-pointed cliffs, if it were not that my purpose in the present work is rather to describe Charles's manner of life than to chronicle the events of the wars that he waged. The sum of this war was the conquest of Italy, the transportation and perpetual exile of King Desiderius, the expulsion of his son Adalgis from Italy, power taken from the kings of the

Lombards and restored to Hadrian, the Ruler of the Roman Church.

7. When this war was ended the Saxon war, which seemed dropped for a time, was taken up again. Never was there a war more prolonged nor more cruel than this, nor one that required greater efforts on the part of the Frankish peoples. For the Saxons, like most of the races that inhabit Germany, are by nature fierce, devoted to the worship of demons and hostile to our religion, and they think it no dishonour to confound and transgress the laws of God and man. There were reasons, too, which might at any time cause a disturbance of the peace. For our boundaries and theirs touch almost everywhere on the open plain, except where in a few places large forests or ranges of mountains are interposed to separate the territories of the two nations by a definite frontier; so that on both sides murder, robbery, and arson were of constant occurrence. The Franks were so irritated by these things that they thought it was time no longer to be satisfied with retaliation but to declare open war against them.

So war was declared, and was fought for thirty years continuously with the greatest fierceness on both sides, but with heavier loss to the Saxons than the Franks. The end might have been reached sooner had it not been for the perfidy of the Saxons. It is hard to say how often they admitted themselves beaten and surrendered as suppliants to King Charles; how often they promised to obey his orders, gave without delay the required hostages, and received the ambassadors that were sent to them. Sometimes they were so cowed and broken that they promised to abandon the worship of devils and willingly to submit themselves to the Christian religion. But though sometimes ready to bow to his commands they were always eager to break their promise, so that it is impossible to say which course seemed to come more natural to them, for from the beginning of the war there was scarcely a year in which they did not both promise and fail to perform.

But the high courage of the King and the constancy of his mind, which remained unshaken by prosperity and adversity, could not be conquered by their changes nor forced by weariness to desist from his undertakings. He never allowed those who offended in this way to go unpunished, but either led an army himself, or sent one under the command of his counts, to chastise their perfidy and inflict a suitable penalty. So that at last, when all who had resisted had been defeated and brought under his power, he took ten thousand of the inhabitants of both banks of the Elbe, with their wives and children, and planted them in many groups in various parts of Germany and Gaul. And at last the war, protracted through so many years, was finished on conditions proposed by the King and accepted by them; they were to abandon the worship of devils, to turn from their national ceremonies, to receive the sacraments of the Christian faith and religion, and then, joined to the Franks, to make one people with them.

8. In this war, despite its prolongation through so many years, he did not himself meet the enemy in battle more than twice—once near the mountain called Osning, in the district of Detmold, and again at the river Hasa—and both these battles were fought in one month, with an interval of only a few days. In these two battles the enemy were so beaten and cowed that they never again ventured to challenge the King nor to resist his attack unless they were protected by some advantage of ground.

In this war many men of noble birth and high office fell on the side both of the Franks and Saxons. But at last it came to an end in the thirty-third year, though in the meanwhile so many and such serious wars broke out against the Franks in all parts of the world, and were carried on with such skill by the King, that an observer may reasonably doubt whether his endurance of toil or his good fortune deserves the greater admiration. For the war in Italy began two years before the Saxon war, and though it was prosecuted without intermission no enterprise in any part of the world was dropped, nor was there anywhere a truce in any struggle, however difficult. For this King, the wisest and most high-minded of all who in that age ruled over the nations of the world, never refused to undertake or prosecute any enterprise because of the labour involved, nor withdrew from it through fear of its danger. He understood the true character of each task that he undertook or carried through, and thus was neither broken by adversity nor misled by the false flatteries of good fortune.

9. Whilst the war with the Saxons was being prosecuted constantly and almost continuously he placed garrisons at suitable places on the frontier, and attacked Spain with the largest military expedition that he could collect. He crossed the Pyrenees, received the surrender of all the towns and fortresses that he attacked, and returned with his army safe and sound, except for a reverse which he experienced through the treason of the Gascons on his return

through the passes of the Pyrenees. For while his army was marching in a long line, suiting their formation to the character of the ground and the defiles, the Gascons placed an ambuscade on the top of the mountain—where the density and extent of the woods in the neighbourhood rendered it highly suitable for such a purpose—and then rushing down into the valley beneath threw into disorder the last part of the baggage train and also the rearguard which acted as a protection to those in advance. In the battle which followed the Gascons slew their opponents to the last man. Then they seized upon the baggage, and under cover of the night, which was already falling, they scattered with the utmost rapidity in different directions. The Gascons were assisted in this feat by the lightness of their armour and the character of the ground where the affair took place. In this battle Eggihard, the surveyor of the royal table; Anselm, the Count of the Palace; and Roland, Præfect of the Breton frontier, were killed along with very many others. Nor could this assault be punished at once, for when the deed had been done the enemy so completely disappeared that they left behind them not so much as a rumour of their whereabouts.

10, He conquered the Bretons, too, who dwelt in

the extreme west of France by the shores of the ocean. They had been disobedient, and he, therefore, sent against them an expedition, by which they were compelled to give hostages and promise that they would henceforth obey his orders.

Then later he himself entered Italy with an army, and, passing through Rome, came to Capua, a city of Campania. There he pitched his camp, and threatened the men of Beneventum with war unless they surrendered. But Aragis, Duke of that people, prevented this war by sending his sons Rumold and Grimold to meet the King with a large sum of money. He asked the King to receive his children as hostages, and promised that he and his people would obey all the commands of the King, except only that he would not come himself into the King's presence. Charles, considering rather the advantage of the people than their Duke's obstinacy, received the hostages who were offered him, and as a great favour consented to forego a personal interview. He kept the younger of the two children as a hostage and sent back the elder one to his father. Then he sent ambassadors to require and receive oaths of fidelity from the Beneventans and from Aragis, and so came back to Rome. There he spent some days in the veneration of the holy places, and then returned to Gaul.

11. Then the Bavarian war broke ou was swiftly ended. It was caused by folly of Tassilo, Duke of Bavaria ; instigation of his wife, who thought that she might revenge through her husband the banishment of her father Desiderius, King of the Lombards, he made an alliance with the Huns, the eastern neighbours of the Bavarians, and not only refused obedience to King Charles but even dared to challenge him in war. The high courage of the King could not bear his overweening insolence, and he forthwith called a general levy for an attack on Bavaria, and came in person with a great army to the river Lech, which separates Bavaria from Germany. He pitched his camp upon the banks of the river, and determined to make trial of the mind of the Duke before he entered the province. But Duke Tassilo saw no profit either for himself or his people in stubbornness, and threw himself upon the King's mercy. He gave the hostages who were demanded, his own son Theodo among the number, and further promised upon oath that no one should ever persuade him again to fall away from his allegiance to the King. And thus a war which seemed likely to grow into a very great one came to a most swift ending. But Tassilo was subsequently summoned into the King's presence, and was not allowed to

[...] province that he ruled was for the [...]ed to the administration not of dukes [...]

[...] these troubles had been settled he waged war against the Slavs, whom we are accustomed to call Wilzi, but who properly—that is, in their own tongue—are called Welatabi. Here the Saxons fought along with the other allied nations who followed the King's standards, though their loyalty was feigned and far from sincere. The cause of the war was that the Wilzi were constantly invading and attacking the Abodriti, the former allies of the Franks, and refused to obey the King's commands to desist from their attacks. There is a gulf stretching from the western sea towards the East, of undiscovered length, but nowhere more than a hundred miles in breadth, and often much narrower. Many nations occupy the shores of this sea. The Danes and the Swedes, whom we call the Northmen, hold its northern shore and all the islands in it. The Slavs and the Aisti and various other nations inhabit the eastern shore, amongst whom the chief are these Welatabi against whom then the King waged war. He so broke and subdued them in a single campaign, conducted by himself, that they thought it no longer wise to refuse to obey his commands.

HUN OR AVAR WAR

13. The greatest of all his wars, next to the Saxon war, followed this one—that, namely, which he undertook against the Huns and the Avars. He prosecuted this with more vigour than the rest and with a far greater military preparation. However, he conducted in person only one expedition into Pannonia, the province then occupied by the Avars; the management of the rest he left to his son Pippin, and the governors of the provinces, and in some cases to his counts and lieutenants. These carried on the war with the greatest energy, and finished it after eight years of fighting. How many battles were fought there and how much blood was shed is still shown by the deserted and uninhabited condition of Pannonia, and the district in which stood the palace of the Kagan is so desolate that there is not so much as a trace of human habitation. All the nobles of the Huns were killed in this war, all their glory passed away; their money and all the treasures that they had collected for so long were carried away. Nor can the memory of man recall any war waged against the Franks by which they were so much enriched and their wealth so increased. Up to this time they were regarded almost as a poor people, but now so much gold and silver were found in the palace, such precious spoils were seized by them in

their battles, that it might fairly be held that the Franks had righteously taken from the Huns what they unrighteously had taken from other nations. Only two of the nobles of the Franks were killed in this war. Eric, the Duke of Friuli, was caught in an ambuscade laid by the townsmen of Tharsatica, a maritime town of Liburnia. And Gerold, the Governor of Bavaria, when he was marshalling his army to fight with the Huns in Pannonia, was killed by an unknown hand, along with two others, who accompanied him as he rode along the line encouraging the soldiers by name. For the rest, the war was almost bloodless so far as the Franks were concerned, and most fortunate in its result although so difficult and protracted.

14. After this the Saxon war ended in a settlement as lasting as the struggle had been protracted. The wars with Bohemia and Luneburg which followed were soon over; both of them were swiftly settled under the command of the younger Charles.

The last war of all that Charles undertook was against those Northmen, who are called Danes, who first came as pirates, and then ravaged the coasts of Gaul and Germany with a greater naval force. Their King, Godofrid, was puffed up with the vain confidence that he would make himself master of all

Germany. He looked upon Frisia and Saxony as his own provinces. He had already reduced his neighbours the Abodriti to obedience, and had forced them to pay him tribute. Now he boasted that he would soon come to Aix, the seat of the King's Court, with a mighty force. His boast, however idle, found some to believe it; it was thought that he would certainly have made some such attempt if he had not been prevented by a sudden death. For he was killed by one of his own followers, and so ended both his life and the war that he had begun.

15. These, then, are the wars which this mighty King waged during the course of forty-seven years—for his reign extended over that period—in different parts of the world with the utmost skill and success. By these wars he so nobly increased the kingdom of the Franks, which was great and strong when he inherited it from his father Pippin, that the additions he made almost doubled it. For before his time the power of the Frankish kingdom extended only over that part of Gaul which is bounded by the Rhine, the Loire, and the Balearic Sea; and that part of Germany which is inhabited by the so-called eastern Franks, and which is bounded by Saxony, the Danube, the Rhine, and the river Saal, which stream

separates the Thuringians and the Sorabs ; and, further, over the Alamanni and the Bavarians. But Charles, by the wars that have been mentioned, conquered and made tributary the following countries :—First, Aquitania and Gascony, and the whole Pyrenean range, and the country of Spain as far as the Ebro, which, rising in Navarre and passing through the most fertile territory of Spain, falls into the Balearic Sea, beneath the walls of the city of Tortosa ; next, all Italy from Augusta Prætoria as far as lower Calabria, where are the frontiers of the Greeks and Beneventans, a thousand miles and more in length ; next, Saxony, which is a considerable portion of Germany, and is reckoned to be twice as broad and about as long as that part of Germany which is inhabited by the Franks ; then both provinces of Pannonia and Dacia, on one side of the river Danube, and Histria and Liburnia and Dalmatia, with the exception of the maritime cities which he left to the Emperor of Constantinople on account of their friendship and the treaty made between them ; lastly, all the barbarous and fierce nations lying between the Rhine, the Vistula, the Ocean, and the Danube, who speak much the same language, but in character and dress are very unlike. The chief of these last are the Welatabi, the Sorabi, the Abodriti, and the Bohemians ;

against these he waged war, but the others, and by far the larger number, surrendered without a struggle.

16. The friendship, too, which he established with certain kings and peoples increased the glory of his reign.

Aldefonsus, King of Gallæcia and Asturica, was joined in so close an alliance with him that whenever he sent letters or ambassadors to Charles he gave instructions that he should be called "the man" of the Frankish King.

Further, his rich gifts had so attached the kings of the Scots to his favour that they always called him their lord and themselves his submissive servants. Letters are still in existence sent by them to Charles in which those feelings towards him are clearly shown.

With Aaron, the King of the Persians, who ruled over all the East, with the exception of India, he entertained so harmonious a friendship that the Persian King valued his favour before the friendship of all the kings and princes in the world, and held that it alone deserved to be cultivated with presents and titles. When, therefore, the ambassadors of Charles, whom he had sent with offerings to the most holy sepulchre of our Lord and Saviour and to the place of His resurrection, came to the Persian King and proclaimed the kindly feelings of their master, he not only granted them all they asked but also allowed that sacred place of our salvation to be reckoned as part of the possessions of the Frankish King. He further sent ambassadors of his own along with those of Charles upon the return journey, and forwarded immense presents to Charles—robes and spices, and the other rich products of the East—and a few years earlier he had sent him at his request an elephant, which was then the only one he had.

The Emperors of Constantinople, Nicephorus, Michael, and Leo, too, made overtures of friendship and alliance with him, and sent many ambassadors. At first Charles was regarded with much suspicion by them, because he had taken the imperial title, and thus seemed to aim at taking from them their empire; but in the end a very definite treaty was made between them, and every occasion of quarrel on either side thereby avoided. For the Romans and the Greeks always suspected the Frankish power; hence there is a well-known Greek proverb: "the Frank is a good friend but a bad neighbour."

17. Though he was so successful in widening the boundaries of his kingdom and subduing the foreign nations he, nevertheless, put on foot many works for the decoration and convenience of his kingdom, and

carried some to completion. The great church dedicated to Mary, the holy Mother of God, at Aix, and the bridge, five hundred feet in length, over the great river Rhine near Mainz, may fairly be regarded as the chief of his works. But the bridge was burnt down a year before his death, and though he had determined to rebuild it of stone instead of wood it was not restored, because his death so speedily followed. He began also to build palaces of splendid workmanship—one not far from the city of Mainz, near a town called Ingelheim; another at Nimeguen, on the river Waal, which flows along the south of the Batavian island. And he gave special orders to the bishops and priests who had charge of sacred buildings that any throughout his realm which had fallen into ruin through age should be restored, and he instructed his agents to see that his orders were carried out.

He built a fleet, too, for the war against the Northmen, constructing ships for this purpose near those rivers which flow out of Gaul and Germany into the northern ocean. And because the Northmen laid waste the coasts of Gaul and Germany by their constant attacks he planted forts and garrisons in all harbours and at the mouths of all navigable rivers, and prevented in this way the passage of the enemy.

He took the same measures in the South, on the shore of Narbonne and Septimania, and also along all the coasts of Italy as far as Rome, to hold in check the Moors, who had lately begun to make piratical excursions. And by reason of these precautions Italy suffered no serious harm from the Moors, nor Gaul and Germany from the Northmen, in the days of Charles; except that Centumcellæ, a city of Etruria, was betrayed into the hands of the Moors and plundered, and in Frisia certain islands lying close to Germany were ravaged by the Northmen.

PART II

PRIVATE LIFE AND CHARACTER OF CHARLEMAGNE

18. I have shown, then, how Charles protected and expanded his kingdom and also what splendour he gave to it. I shall now go on to speak of his mental endowments, of his steadiness of purpose under whatever circumstances of prosperity or adversity, and of all that concerns his private and domestic life.

As long as, after the death of his father, he shared the kingdom with his brother he bore so patiently the quarrelling and restlessness of the latter as never even to be provoked to wrath by him. Then, having married at his mother's bidding the daughter of Desiderius, King of the Lombards, he divorced her, for some unknown reason, a year later. He took in marriage Hildigard, of the Suabian race, a woman of the highest nobility, and by her he had three sons —viz. Charles and Pippin and Ludovicus, and three daughters—Hrotrud and Bertha and Gisla. He had also three other daughters—Theoderada and Hiltrud and Hruodhaid. Two of these were the children of his wife Fastrada, a woman of the eastern Franks or Germans; the third was the daughter of a concubine, whose name has escaped my memory. On the death of Fastrada he married Liutgard, of the Alemannic race, by whom he had no children. After her death he had four concubines—namely, Madelgarda, who bore him a daughter of the name of Ruothild; Gersuinda, of Saxon origin, by whom he had a daughter of the name of Adolthrud; Regina, who bore him Drogot and Hugo; and Adallinda, who was the mother of Theoderic.

His mother Bertrada lived with him to old age in great honour. He treated her with the utmost reverence, so that no quarrel of any kind ever arose between them—except in the matter of the divorce of the daughter of King Desiderius, whom he had married at her bidding. Bertrada died after the death of Hildigard, having lived to see three grandsons and as many granddaughters in her son's house. Charles had his mother buried with great honour in the same great church of St Denys in which his father lay.

He had only one sister, Gisla, who from childhood

was dedicated to the religious life. He treated her with the same affectionate respect as his mother. She died a few years before Charles's own death in the monastery in which she had passed her life.

19. In educating his children he determined to train them, both sons and daughters, in those liberal studies to which he himself paid great attention. Further, he made his sons, as soon as their age permitted it, learn to ride like true Franks, and practise the use of arms and hunting. He ordered his daughters to learn wool work and devote attention to the spindle and distaff, for the avoidance of idleness and lethargy, and to be trained to the adoption of high principles.

He lost two sons and one daughter before his death—namely, Charles, his eldest; Pippin, whom he made King of Italy; and Hruotrud, his eldest daughter, who had been betrothed to Constantine, the Emperor of the Greeks. Pippin left one son, Bernard, and five daughters—Adalheid, Atula, Gundrada, Berthaid, and Theoderada. In his treatment of them Charles gave the strongest proof of his family affection, for upon the death of his son he appointed his grandson Bernard to succeed him, and had his granddaughters brought up with his own daughters.

He bore the deaths of his two sons and of his

daughters with less patience than might have been expected from his usual stoutness of heart, for his domestic affection, a quality for which he was as remarkable as for courage, forced him to shed tears. Moreover, when the death of Hadrian, the Roman Pontiff, whom he reckoned as the chief of his friends, was announced to him, he wept for him as though he had lost a brother or a very dear son. For he showed a very fine disposition in his friendships: he embraced them readily and maintained them faithfully, and he treated with the utmost respect all whom he had admitted into the circle of his friends.

He had such care of the upbringing of his sons and daughters that he never dined without them when he was at home, and never travelled without them. His sons rode along with him, and his daughters followed in the rear. Some of his guards, chosen for this very purpose, watched the end of the line of march where his daughters travelled. They were very beautiful, and much beloved by their father, and, therefore, it is strange that he would give them in marriage to no one, either among his own people or of a foreign state. But up to his death he kept them all at home, saying that he could not forego their society. And hence the good fortune that followed him in all other respects was here broken by the touch of scandal and failure. He shut his eyes, however, to everything, and acted as though no suspicion of anything amiss had reached him, or as if the rumour of it had been discredited.

20. He had by a concubine a son called Pippin—whom I purposely did not mention along with the others — handsome, indeed, but deformed. When Charles, after the beginning of the war against the Huns, was wintering in Bavaria, this Pippin pretended illness, and formed a conspiracy against his father with some of the leaders of the Franks, who had seduced him by a vain promise of the kingdom. When the design had been detected and the conspirators punished Pippin was tonsured and sent to the monastery of Prumia, there to practise the religious life, to which in the end he was of his own will inclined.

Another dangerous conspiracy had been formed against him in Germany at an earlier date. The plotters were some of them blinded and some of them maimed, and all subsequently transported into exile. Not more than three lost their lives, and these resisted capture with drawn swords, and in defending themselves killed some of their opponents. Hence, as they could not be restrained in any other way, they were cut down.

The cruelty of Queen Fastrada is believed to be

the cause and origin of these conspiracies. Both were caused by the belief that, upon the persuasion of his cruel wife, he had swerved widely from his natural kindness and customary leniency. Otherwise his whole life long he so won the love and favour of all men both at home and abroad that never was the slightest charge of unjust severity brought against him by anyone.

21. He had a great love for foreigners, and took such pains to entertain them that their numbers were justly reckoned to be a burden not only to the palace but to the kingdom at large. But, with his usual loftiness of spirit, he took little note of such charges, for he found in the reputation of generosity and in the good fame that followed such actions a compensation even for grave inconveniences.

22. His body was large and strong; his stature tall but not ungainly, for the measure of his height was seven times the length of his own feet. The top of his head was round; his eyes were very large and piercing. His nose was rather larger than is usual; he had beautiful white hair; and his expression was brisk and cheerful; so that, whether sitting or standing, his appearance was dignified and impressive. Although his neck was rather thick and short and he was somewhat corpulent this was not noticed owing

to the good proportions of the rest of his body. His step was firm and the whole carriage of his body manly; his voice was clear, but hardly so strong as you would have expected. He had good health, but for four years before his death was frequently attacked by fevers, and at last was lame of one foot. Even then he followed his own opinion rather than the advice of his doctors, whom he almost hated, because they advised him to give up the roast meat to which he was accustomed, and eat boiled instead. He constantly took exercise both by riding and hunting. This was a national habit; for there is hardly any race on the earth that can be placed on equality with the Franks in this respect. He took delight in the vapour of naturally hot waters, and constantly practised swimming, in which he was so proficient that no one could be fairly regarded as his superior. Partly for this reason he built his palace at Aix, and lived there continuously during the last years of his life up to the time of his death. He used to invite not only his sons to the bath but also his nobles and friends, and at times even a great number of his followers and bodyguards.

23. He wore the national—that is to say, the Frankish dress. His shirts and drawers were of linen, then came a tunic with a silken fringe, and hose. His legs were cross-gartered and his feet enclosed in shoes.

In winter-time he defended his shoulders and chest with a jerkin made of the skins of otters and ermine. He was clad in a blue cloak, and always wore a sword, with the hilt and belt of either gold or silver. Occasionally, too, he used a jewelled sword, but this was only on the great festivals or when he received ambassadors from foreign nations. He disliked foreign garments, however beautiful, and would never consent to wear them, except once at Rome on the request of Pope Hadrian, and once again upon the entreaty of his successor, Pope Leo, when he wore a long tunic and cloak, and put on shoes made after the Roman fashion. On festal days he walked in procession in a garment of gold cloth, with jewelled boots and a golden girdle to his cloak, and distinguished further by a diadem of gold and precious stones. But on other days his dress differed little from that of the common people.

24. He was temperate in eating and drinking, but especially so in drinking; for he had a fierce hatred of drunkenness in any man, and especially in himself or in his friends. He could not abstain so easily from food, and used often to complain that fasting was injurious to his health. He rarely gave large banquets, and only on the high festivals, but then he invited a large number of guests. His daily meal was served in four courses only, exclusive of the roast,

which the hunters used to bring in on spits, and which he ate with more pleasure than any other food. During the meal there was either singing or a reader for him to listen to. Histories and the great deeds of men of old were read to him. He took delight also in the books of Saint Augustine, and especially in those which are entitled the City of God. He was so temperate in the use of wine and drink of any kind that he rarely drank oftener than thrice during dinner.

In summer, after his midday meal, he took some fruit and a single draught, and then, taking off his clothes and boots, just as he was accustomed to do at night, he would rest for two or three hours. At night he slept so lightly that he would wake, and even rise, four or five times during the night.

When he was putting on his boots and clothes he not only admitted his friends, but if the Count of the Palace told him there was any dispute which could not be settled without his decision he would have the litigants at once brought in, and hear the case, and pronounce on it just as if he were sitting on the tribunal. He would, moreover, at the same time transact any business that had to be done that day or give any orders to his servants.

25. In speech he was fluent and ready, and could

express with the greatest clearness whatever he wished. He was not merely content with his native tongue but took the trouble to learn foreign languages. He learnt Latin so well that he could speak it as well as his native tongue ; but he could understand Greek better than he could speak it. His fluency of speech was so great that he even seemed sometimes a little garrulous.

He paid the greatest attention to the liberal arts, and showed the greatest respect and bestowed high honours upon those who taught them. For his lessons in grammar he listened to the instruction of Deacon Peter of Pisa, an old man ; but for all other subjects Albinus, called Alcuin, also a deacon, was his teacher—a man from Britain, of the Saxon race, and the most learned man of his time. Charles spent much time and labour in learning rhetoric and dialectic, and especially astronomy, from Alcuin. He learnt, too, the art of reckoning, and with close application scrutinised most carefully the course of the stars. He tried also to learn to write, and for this purpose used to carry with him and keep under the pillow of his couch tablets and writing-sheets that he might in his spare moments accustom himself to the formation of letters. But he made little advance in this strange task, which was begun too late in life.

CARE FOR RELIGION

26. He paid the most devout and pious regard to the Christian religion, in which he had been brought up from infancy. And, therefore, he built the great and most beautiful church at Aix, and decorated it with gold and silver and candelabras and with wicket-gates and doors of solid brass. And, since he could not procure marble columns elsewhere for the building of it, he had them brought from Rome and Ravenna. As long as his health permitted it he used diligently to attend the church both in the morning and evening, and during the night, and at the time of the Sacrifice. He took the greatest care to have all the services of the church performed with the utmost dignity, and constantly warned the keepers of the building not to allow anything improper or dirty either to be brought into or to remain in the building. He provided so great a quantity of gold and silver vessels, and so large a supply of priestly vestments, that at the religious services not even the door-keepers, who form the lowest ecclesiastical order, had to officiate in their ordinary dress. He carefully reformed the manner of reading and singing; for he was thoroughly instructed in both, though he never read publicly himself, nor sang except in a low voice, and with the rest of the congregation.

27. He was most devout in relieving the poor and

in those free gifts which the Greeks call alms. For he gave it his attention not only in his own country and in his own kingdom, but he also used to send money across the sea to Syria, to Egypt, to Africa—to Jerusalem, Alexandria, and Carthage—in compassion for the poverty of any Christians whose miserable condition in those countries came to his ears. It was for this reason chiefly that he cultivated the friendship of kings beyond the sea, hoping thereby to win for the Christians living beneath their sway some succour and relief.

Beyond all other sacred and venerable places he loved the church of the holy Apostle Peter at Rome, and he poured into its treasury great wealth in silver and gold and precious stones. He sent innumerable gifts to the Pope; and during the whole course of his reign he strove with all his might (and, indeed, no object was nearer to his heart than this) to restore to the city of Rome her ancient authority, and not merely to defend the church of Saint Peter but to decorate and enrich it out of his resources above all other churches. But although he valued Rome so much, still, during all the forty-seven years that he reigned, he only went there four times to pay his vows and offer up his prayers.

28. But such were not the only objects of his last

visit; for the Romans had grievously outraged Pope Leo, had torn out his eyes and cut off his tongue, and thus forced him to throw himself upon the protection of the King. He, therefore came to Rome to restore the condition of the church, which was terribly disturbed, and spent the whole of the winter there. It was then that he received the title of Emperor and Augustus, which he so disliked at first that he affirmed that he would not have entered the church on that day—though it was the chief festival of the church—if he could have foreseen the design of the Pope. But when he had taken the title he bore very quietly the hostility that it caused and the indignation of the Roman emperors. He conquered their ill-feeling by his magnanimity, in which, doubtless, he far excelled them, and sent frequent embassies to them, and called them his brothers.

29. When he had taken the imperial title he noticed many defects in the legal systems of his people; for the Franks have two legal systems, differing in many points very widely from one another, and he, therefore, determined to add what was lacking, to reconcile the differences, and to amend anything that was wrong or wrongly expressed. He completed nothing of all his designs beyond adding a few capitularies, and those unfinished. But he gave orders

that the laws and rules of all nations comprised within his dominions which were not already written out should be collected and committed to writing.

He also wrote out the barbarous and ancient songs, in which the acts of the kings and their wars were sung, and committed them to memory. He also began a grammar of his native language.

He gave the months names in his own tongue, for before his time they were called by the Franks partly by Latin and partly by barbarous names. He also gave names to the twelve winds, whereas before not more than four, and perhaps not so many, had names of their own. Of the months, he called January Winter-month, February Mud-month, March Spring-month, April Easter-month, May Joy-month, June Plough-month, July Hay-month, August Harvest-month, September Wind-month, October Vintage-month, November Autumn-month, December Holy-month. The following are the names which he gave to the winds:—The Subsolanus (east) he called East Wind; the Eurus (east by south) East-South Wind; the Euroauster (south by east) South-East Wind; the Auster (south) South Wind; the Austro-Afric (south by west) South-West Wind; the Afric (west by south) West-South Wind; the Zephyr (west) West Wind; the Corus (west by north) West-North

Wind; the Circius (north by west) North-West Wind; the Septentrion (north) North Wind; the Aquilon (north by east) North-East Wind; the Vulturnus (east by north) East-North Wind.

30. At the very end of his life, when already he was feeling the pressure of old age and sickness, he summoned his own son Lewis, King of Aquitania, the only surviving son of Hildigard, and then solemnly called together the Frankish nobles of his whole kingdom; and then, with the consent of all, made Lewis partner in the whole kingdom and heir to the imperial title. After that, putting the diadem on his head, he ordered them to salute him "Imperator" and Augustus. This decision of his was received by all present with the greatest favour, for it seemed to them a divine inspiration for the welfare of the realm. It added to his dignity at home and increased the terror of his name abroad.

He then sent his son back to Aquitania, and himself, though broken with old age, proceeded to hunt, as his custom was, not far from the palace of Aix, and after spending the rest of the autumn in this pursuit he came back to Aix about the beginning of November. Whilst he was spending the winter there he was attacked by a sharp fever, and took to his bed. Then, following his usual habit, he determined to abstain from food, thinking that by such self-discipline he would be able either to cure or alleviate the disease. But the fever was complicated by a pain in the side which the Greeks call pleurisy ; and, as Charles still persisted in fasting, and only very rarely drank something to sustain his strength, seven days after he had taken to his bed he received holy communion, and died, in the seventy-second year of his life and in the forty-seventh year of his reign, on the fifth day before the Kalends of February, at the third hour of the day.

31. His body was washed and treated with the usual ceremonies, and then, amidst the greatest grief of the whole people, taken to the church and buried. At first there was some doubt as to where he should rest, since he had given no instructions during his lifetime. But at length all were agreed that he could be buried nowhere more honourably than in the great church which he had built at his own expense in the same town, for the love of our Lord God Jesus Christ and the honour of His holy and ever-virgin Mother. There he was buried on the same day on which he died. A gilded arch was raised above the tomb, with his statue, and an inscription. The inscription ran as follows :—

"Beneath this tomb lies the body of Charles, the great and orthodox Emperor, who nobly expanded the kingdom of the Franks and reigned prosperously for forty-seven years. He departed this life, more than seventy years of age, in the eight hundred and fourteenth year of our Lord, in the seventh indiction, on the fifth day before the Kalends of February."

32. There were many prodigies to show that his end drew near, and he as well as others understood the meaning of their warnings. During all the three last years of his life there were constant eclipses of sun and moon, and a black coloured spot appeared in the sun for the space of seven days. The gallery which he had built, of great size and strength, between the palace and the church, suddenly, on Ascension Day, fell in ruins down even to the foundations. Also, the wooden bridge over the Rhine near Mainz, which he had built with wonderful skill, and the labour of ten years, so that it seemed as though it would last for ever, was accidentally set on fire, and in three hours burnt so far that not a plank remained except those that were covered by the water. Further, when he was making his last expedition in Saxony against Godofrid, King of the Danes, as he was moving

out of camp and beginning his march before sunrise, he suddenly saw a meteor rush across the heavens with a great blaze and pass from right to left through the clear sky. Whilst all were wondering what this sign meant, suddenly the horse that he was riding fell head foremost, and threw him so violently to the ground that the girdle of his cloak was broken, and his sword belt slipped from it. When his attendants ran up to help him they found him disarmed and disrobed. His javelin, too, which he was holding in his hand at the time of his fall, fell twenty paces and more away from him. Moreover, the palace at Aix was frequently shaken, and in houses where he lived there was a constant creaking in the fretted ceilings. The church in which he was afterwards buried was struck by lightning, and the golden apple that adorned the summit of the roof was thrown down by a thunder-stroke, and fell upon the Bishop's house, which adjoined the church. In the same church an inscription was written on the edge of the circular space which ran round the inside of the church between the upper and lower arches, saying by whom the sacred edifice had been built. And in the last line occurred the words: "Carolus Princeps." Some noticed that in the very year in which Charles died, and a few months before his death, the letters of the word "princeps" were so destroyed as to be quite invisible. But he either refused to notice or despised all these omens as though they had no connection at all with anything that concerned him.

33. He had determined to draw out wills in order to make his daughters and the sons whom his concubines had borne to him heirs to some part of his property; but he took up this design too late, and could not carry it out. But some three years before he died he divided his treasures, his money and his robes, and all his other moveable property, in presence of his friends and ministers, and appealed to them to ratify and maintain by their support this division after his death. He also stated in a document how he wished to have the property which he had divided disposed of. The text and purport of the document ran as follows:—

In the name of the Lord God Almighty, Father, Son, and Holy Ghost. This is the description and division which was made by the most glorious and pious lord Charles, the august Emperor, in the eight hundred and eleventh year from the incarnation of our Lord Jesus Christ; in the forty-third year of his reign in Frankland; in the thirty-sixth year of his reign in Italy; in the eleventh year of his Empire and in the fourth indiction: which division he made for wise and religious reasons of his treasures and of the money which on that day was found in the treasury. Wherein his great aim was: in the first place to ensure that the distribution of alms, which Christians religiously make from their possessions, should be duly and properly made on his account from his wealth; and also that his heirs may clearly know without any possibility of doubt what ought to belong to them, and may therefore (without contest or dissension) divide his goods among themselves in their proper proportion. Therefore with this intention and object he first divided into three parts all his property and moveable goods; which, whether consisting of gold, silver, jewels, or royal apparel, could be found on the afore-mentioned day in his treasury. Then, by a further distribution, he divided two of those three parts into twenty-one parts, and kept the third part undivided.

The distribution of the two parts into twenty-one is to be carried out in the following way. As there are known to be twenty-one metropolitan cities in his realm, one of those twenty-one parts is to be handed over to each metropolitan city by his heirs and friends for the purpose of almsgiving. The Archbishop who at the time of his death is ruling the metropolitan sees shall receive that part for his church and divide it among his suffragans; one-third going to his own church and two-thirds being divided among his suffragans.

Each of these divisions—which, as already mentioned, are made out of the first two-thirds, and are twenty-one in number, according to the number of the metropolitan sees—is separated from the rest and put away by itself in a repository of its own with the title of the city attached to which it is to be given. The names of the metropolitan sees, to which this alms or largess is to be given, are Rome, Ravenna, Milan, Fréjus, Grado, Cologne, Mainz, Juvavum which is also called Salsburg, Trèves, Sens, Besançon, Lyons, Rouen, Rheims, Arles, Vienne, Darantasia, Embrun, Bordeaux, Tours, Bourges.

The following disposition shall be made of the one part hitherto left undivided. When the first two parts have been distributed into the before-mentioned divisions, and have been put away under seal, this third part shall be employed for daily uses, as not being alienated by any bond or promise of the owner; and it shall be so used as long as he himself remains in the flesh or judges its employment to be necessary to him. But after his death or his voluntary retirement from the affairs of the world that part shall be divided into four subdivisions. Of these subdivisions one shall be added to the before-mentioned twenty-one parts ; the second shall be taken by his sons and daughters, and by the sons and daughters of his sons, and shall be divided among them in just and reasonable proportion ; the third shall be devoted to the use of the poor in the manner usual among Christians ; the fourth part shall similarly be divided for alms and go to the support of the servants, both men and women, who attend to the needs of the palaces.

He desired further that there should be added to this third part of the total sum, which like the other parts consists of gold and silver, all vessels and utensils of brass, iron or other metals, with arms, clothes and all other moveable articles, whether of value or not, which are employed for various purposes ; as for instance curtains, coverlets, tapestries, woollen-cloths, dressed-skins, harnesses, and whatever else is found at that date in his store chamber or wardrobe : so that in this way the subdivisions of that part may be larger, and the distribution of alms find its way to a larger number.

He desired that the chapel—that is, the materials

for the service of the church, both those which he himself gave and collected and those which came to him by inheritance from his father—should remain entire and suffer no division of any kind. But if any vessel or books or other ornaments are found, which have certainly not been given by him to the aforementioned chapel, these may be bought and possessed by anyone who wants them, at a price fixed by a reasonable valuation. He similarly determined that the books, of which he had collected a great quantity in his library, should be sold at a reasonable price to anyone who wanted them and the money handed over to the poor. Amongst his treasures there are three tables of silver and one of gold of remarkable size and weight. Concerning these he determined and decided as follows. One of them, square in shape, containing a map of the city of Constantinople, shall be sent to Rome for the cathedral of the holy Apostle Peter, along with the other gifts which are set aside for that purpose. The second, round in shape, inscribed with a picture of the city of Rome, shall be given to the Bishopric of the Church of Ravenna. The third, which is far superior to the others both in beauty of workmanship and in weight, which is made of three circles, and contains a map of the whole world, skilfully and minutely drawn, shall go to increase that third part which is to be divided among his heirs and given in alms.

This disposition and arrangement he made and drew up in presence of the bishops, abbots and counts, who could then be present and whose names are here written out.

Bishops

Hildibald
Richolf
Arno
Wolphar
Bernoin
Laidrad
John
Theodolf
Jesse
Heito
Waltgaud

Abbots

Fridugisius
Adalung
Engilbert
Irmin

Counts

Walatho
Meginher
Otolf
Stephen
Unruoc
Barchard
Meginhard
Hatto
Rihwin
Edo
Ercangar
Gerold
Bero
Hildigern
Roccolf

HIS WILL EXECUTED

His son Lewis, who by the designs of Providence succeeded him, inspected the aforesaid document, and carried out these arrangements with the greatest devotion immediately after his death.

THE LIFE OF CHARLEMAGNE BY THE MONK OF ST GALL

BOOK I

CONCERNING THE PIETY OF CHARLES AND HIS CARE OF THE CHURCH

AFTER the omnipotent ruler of the world, who orders alike the fate of kingdoms and the course of time, had broken the feet of iron and clay in one noble statue, to wit the Romans, he raised by the hands of the illustrious Charles the golden head of another, not less admirable, among the Franks. Now it happened, when he had begun to reign alone in the western parts of the world, and the pursuit of learning had been almost forgotten throughout all his realm, and the worship of the true Godhead was faint and weak, that two Scots came from Ireland to the coast of Gaul along with certain traders of Britain. These Scotchmen were unrivalled for their skill in sacred and secular learning: and day by day, when the crowd gathered round them for traffic, they exhibited no wares for sale, but cried out and said,

"Ho, everyone that desires wisdom, let him draw near and take it at our hands; for it is wisdom that we have for sale."

Now they declared that they had wisdom for sale because they said that the people cared not for what was given freely but only for what was sold, hoping that thus they might be incited to purchase wisdom along with other wares; and also perhaps hoping that by this announcement they themselves might become a wonder and a marvel to men: which indeed turned out to be the case. For so long did they make their proclamation that in the end those who wondered at these men, or perhaps thought them insane, brought the matter to the ears of King Charles, who always loved and sought after wisdom. Wherefore he ordered them to come with all speed into his presence and asked them whether it were true, as fame reported of them, that they had brought wisdom with them. They answered, "We both possess it and are ready to give it, in the name of God, to those who seek it worthily." Again he asked them what price they asked for it; and they answered, "We ask no price, O king; but we ask only for a fit place for teaching and quick minds to teach; and besides food to eat and raiment to put on, for without these we cannot accomplish our pilgrimage."

L 7

This answer filled the king with a great joy, and first he kept both of them with him for a short time. But soon, when he must needs go to war, he made one of them named Clement reside in Gaul, and to him he sent many boys both of noble, middle and humble birth, and he ordered as much food to be given them as they required, and he set aside for them buildings suitable for study. But he sent the second scholar into Italy and gave him the monastery of Saint Augustine near Pavia, that all who wished might gather there to learn from him.

2. But when Albinus (Alcuin), an Englishman, heard that that most religious Emperor Charles gladly entertained wise men, he entered into a ship and came to him. Now Albinus was skilled in all learning beyond all others of our times, for he was the disciple of that most learned priest Bede, who next to Saint Gregory was the most skilful interpreter of the scriptures. And Charles received Albinus kindly and kept him at his side to the end of his life, except when he marched with his armies to his vast wars: nay, Charles would even call himself Albinus's disciple; and Albinus he would call his master. He appointed him to rule over the abbey of Saint Martin, near to the city of Tours: so that, when he himself was absent, Albinus might rest there and

teach those who had recourse to him. And his teaching bore such fruit among his pupils that the modern Gauls or Franks came to equal the ancient Romans or Athenians.

3. Then when Charles came back, after a long absence, crowned with victory, into Gaul, he ordered the boys whom he had entrusted to Clement to come before him and present to him letters and verses of their own composition. Now the boys of middle or low birth presented him with writings garnished with the sweet savours of wisdom beyond all that he could have hoped, while those of the children of noble parents were silly and tasteless. Then the most wise Charles, imitating the judgment of the eternal Judge, gathered together those who had done well upon his right hand and addressed them in these words: "My children, you have found much favour with me because you have tried with all your strength to carry out my orders and win advantage for yourselves. Wherefore now study to attain to perfection; and I will give you bishoprics and splendid monasteries, and you shall be always honourable in my eyes." Then he turned severely to those who were gathered on his left, and, smiting their consciences with the fire of his eyes, he flung at them in scorn these terrible words, which seemed thunder rather

than human speech, "You nobles, you sons of my chiefs, you superfine dandies, you have trusted to your birth and your possessions and have set at naught my orders to your own advancement: you have neglected the pursuit of learning and you have given yourselves over to luxury and sport, to idleness and profitless pastimes." Then solemnly he raised his august head and his unconquered right hand to the heavens and thus thundered against them, "By the King of Heaven, I take no account of your noble birth and your fine looks, though others may admire you for them. Know this for certain, that unless you make up for your former sloth by vigorous study, you will never get any favour from Charles."

4. Charles used to pick out all the best writers and readers from among the poor boys that I have spoken of and transferred them to his chapel; for that was the name that the kings of the Franks gave to their private oratory, taking the word from the *cope* of St Martin, which they always took with them in war for a defence against their enemies. Now one day it was announced to this most wary King Charles that a certain bishop was dead; and, when the king asked whether the dead bishop had made any bequests for the good of his soul, the messenger replied, "Sire, he has bequeathed no more than two pounds of silver."

Thereupon one of his chaplains, sighing, and no longer able to keep the thoughts of his mind within his breast, spake in the hearing of the king these words: "That is a small provision for a long, a never-ending journey."

Then Charles, the mildest of men, deliberated a space, and said to the young man, "Do you think then, if you were to get the bishopric, you would care to make more provision for that same long journey?" These cautious words fell upon the chaplain as ripe grapes into the mouth of one who stands agape for them, and he threw himself at the feet of Charles and said, "Sire, the matter rests upon the will of God and your own power." Said the king, "Stand behind the curtain, that hangs behind me, and mark what kind of help you would receive if you were raised to that honour."

Now, when the officers of the palace, who were always on the watch for deaths or accidents, heard that the bishop was dead, one and all of them, impatient of delay and jealous of each other, began to make suit for the bishopric through the friends of the emperor. But Charles still persisted unmoved in his design; he refused everyone, and said that he would not disappoint his young friend. At last Queen Hildigard sent some of the nobles of the realm, and at last came in person, to beg the bishopric for a certain clerk of her own. The emperor received her petition very graciously and said that he would not and could not deny her anything; but that he thought it shame to deceive his little chaplain. But still the queen, woman-like, thought that a woman's opinion and wish ought to outweigh the decrees of men; and so she concealed the passion that was rising in her heart; she sank her strong voice almost to a whisper; and with caressing gestures tried to soften the emperor's unspoken mind. "My sire and king," she said, "what does it matter if that boy does lose the bishopric? Nay, I beseech you, sweet sire, my glory and my refuge, give it to your faithful servant, my clerk." Then that young man, who had heard the petitions from behind the curtain close to the king's chair where he had been placed, embraced the king through the curtain and cried, "Sir king, stand fast and do not let anyone take from you the power that has been given you by God."

Then that strict lover of truth bade him come out, and said, "I intend you to have the bishopric; but you must be very careful to spend more and make fuller provision for that same long and unreturning journey both for yourself and for me."

5. Now there was at the king's court a certain

mean and humble clerk, very deficient also in a knowledge of letters. The most pious Charles pitied his poverty, and, though everyone hated him and tried to drive him from the court, he could never be persuaded to turn him away or dismiss him therefrom. Now it happened that, on the eve of Saint Martin, the death of a certain bishop was announced to the emperor. He summoned one of his clerks, a man of high birth and great learning, and gave him the bishopric. The new bishop, thereupon, bursting with joy, invited to his house many of the palace attendants, and also received with great pomp many who came from the diocese to greet him: and to all he gave a superb banquet.

It happened then that, loaded with food, drenched with liquor and buried in wine, he failed to go to the evening service on that most solemn eve. Now it was the custom for the chief of the choir to assign the day before to everyone the responsory or responsories which they were to chant at night. The response: *Lord, if still I am useful to Thy people,* had fallen to the lot of this man, who had the bishopric, as it were, in his grasp. Well, he was absent; and after the lesson a long pause followed, and each man urged his neighbour to take up the responsory, and each man answered that he was bound to chant only what had been assigned to him. At last the emperor said: "Come, one of you must chant it." Then this mean clerk, strengthened by some divine inspiration, and encouraged by the command, took upon himself the responsory. The kindly king thinking that he would not be able to chant the whole of it ordered the others to help him and all began at once to chant. But from none of them could the poor creature learn the words, and, when the response was finished, he began to chant the Lord's Prayer with the proper intonation. Then everyone wished to stop him; but the most wise Charles wanted to see where he would get to, and forbade anyone to interfere with him. He finished with *Thy Kingdom come* and the rest, willy-willy, had to take it up and say *Thy will be done*.

When the early lauds were finished, the king went back to his palace, or rather to his bedroom, to warm himself and dress for the coming festal ceremony. He ordered that miserable servant and unpractised chanter to come into his presence. "Who told you to chant that responsory?" he asked. "Sire, you ordered someone to sing," said the other. "Well," said the king (the emperor was called king at first), "who told you to begin in that particular responsory?" Then the poor creature, inspired as it is thought by

God, spoke as follows, in the fashion which inferiors then used to superiors, whether for honour, appeal, or flattery :—"Blessed lord, and blessing-bestowing king, as I could not find out the right verse from anyone, I said to myself that I should incur the anger of your majesty if I introduced anything strange. So I determined to intone something the latter part of which usually came at the end of the responsories."

The kindly emperor smiled gently upon him and thus spoke before all his nobles. "That proud man, who neither feared nor honoured God or his king who had befriended him, enough to refrain one night from dissipation and be in his place to chant the response which I am told fell to his share, is by God's decree and mine deprived of his bishopric. You shall take it, for God gives it you, and I allow it ; and be sure to administer it according to canonical and apostolic rules."

6. When another prince of the Church died, the emperor appointed a young man in his place. When the bishop designate came out of the palace to take his departure, his servants, with all the decorum that was due to a bishop, brought forward a horse and steps to mount it : but he took it amiss that they should treat him as though he were decrepit ; and leaped from the ground on to the horse's back with such violence that

he nearly fell off on the other side. The king looked on from the steps of the palace and had him summoned and thus addressed him : " My good sir, you are nimble and quick, agile and headstrong. You know yourself that the calm of our empire is disturbed on all sides by the tempests of many wars. Wherefore I want a priest like you at my court. Remain therefore as an associate in my labours as long as you can mount your horse with such agility."

7. While I was speaking about the arrangement of the responses I forgot to speak about the rules for reading and I must devote a few words to that subject here. In the palace of the most learned Charles there was no one to apportion to each reader the passages that were to be read ; no one put a seal at the end of the passage or made ever such a little mark with his finger-nail. But all had to make themselves so well acquainted with the passage, which was set down for reading, that if they were suddenly called on to read they could perform their duty without incurring his censure. He indicated whom he wished to read by pointing his finger or his staff, or by sending some one of those who were sitting close by him to those at a distance. He marked the end of the reading by a guttural sound. And all watched so intently for this mark that whether it came at the end of a sentence

or in the middle of a clause or a sub-clause, none dared go on for an instant, however strange the beginning or the end might seem. And thus it came to pass that all in the palace were excellent readers, even if they did not understand what they read. No foreigner and no celebrity dared enter his choir unless he could read and chant.

8. When Charles one day came in his journeyings to a certain palace, a certain clerk from among the wandering monks entered the choir and being completely ignorant of these rules was soon forced to remain stupid and silent among the singers. Thereupon the choirmaster raised his wand and threatened to strike him unless he went on singing. Then the poor clerk, not knowing what to do or where to turn, and not daring to go out, twisted his neck into the shape of a bow and with open mouth and distended cheeks did his utmost to imitate the appearance of a singer. All the rest could not restrain their laughter, but the most valiant emperor, whose mind was never shaken from its firm base even by great events, seemed not to notice his mockery of singing and waited in due order until the end of the mass. But then he called the poor wretch before him and pitying his struggles and his anxiety soothed his fears with these words :—"Many thanks, good clerk, for your singing and your

efforts." Then he ordered a pound of silver to be given him to relieve his poverty.

9. But I must not seem to forget or to neglect Alcuin; and will therefore make this true statement about his energy and his deserts: all his pupils without exception distinguished themselves by becoming either holy abbots or bishops. My master Grimald studied the literal arts under him, first in Gaul and then in Italy. But those who are learned in these matters may charge me with falsehood for saying "all his pupils without exception"; when the fact is that there were in his schools two young men, sons of a miller in the service of the monastery of Saint Columban, who did not seem fit and proper persons for promotion to the command of bishoprics or monasteries; but even these men were, by the influence probably of their teacher, advanced one after the other to the office of minister in the monastery of Bobbio, in which they displayed the greatest energy.

So the most glorious Charles saw the study of letters flourishing throughout his whole realm, but still he was grieved to find that it did not reach the ripeness of the earlier fathers; and so, after superhuman labours, he broke out one day with this expression of his sorrow: "Would that I had twelve clerks so learned in all wisdom and so perfectly trained as were Jerome and Augustine." Then the learned Alcuin, feeling himself ignorant indeed in comparison with these great names, rose to a height of daring, that no man else attained to in the presence of the terrible Charles, and said, with deep indignation in his mind but none in his countenance, "The Maker of heaven and earth has not many like to those men and do you expect to have twelve?"

10. Here I must report something which the men of our time will find it difficult to believe; for I myself who write it could hardly believe it, so great is the difference between our method of chanting and the Roman, were it not that we must trust rather the accuracy of our fathers than the false suggestions of modern sloth. Well then, Charles, that never-wearied lover of the service of God, when he could congratulate himself that all possible progress had been made in the knowledge of letters, was grieved to observe how widely the different provinces—nay, not the provinces only but districts and cities—differed in the praise of God, that is to say in their method of chanting. He therefore asked of Pope Stephen of blessed memory—the same who, after Hilderich King of the Franks had been deposed and tonsured, had anointed Charles to be ruler of the kingdom after the ancestral custom of the people—he asked

of Pope Stephen, I say, that he should provide him with twelve clerks deeply learned in divine song. The Pope yielded assent to his virtuous wish and his divinely inspired design and sent to him in Frankland from the apostolic see clerks skilled in divine song, and twelve in number, according to the number of the twelve apostles.

Now, when I said Frankland just above, I meant all the provinces north of the Alps; for as it is written: "In those days ten men shall take hold out of all the languages of the nations, shall even take hold of the skirt of him that is a Jew," so at that time, by reason of the glory of Charles, Gauls, Aquitanians, Æduans, Spaniards, Germans, and Bavarians thought that no small honour was paid to them, if they were thought worthy to be called the servants of the Franks.

Now when the aforementioned clerks were departing from Rome, being, like all Greeks and Romans, torn with envy of the glory of the Franks, they took counsel among themselves, and determined so to vary their method of singing that his kingdom and dominion should never have cause to rejoice in unity and agreement. So when they came to Charles they were received most honourably and despatched to the chief places. And thereupon each in his allotted place began to chant as differently as possible, and to teach others to sing in like fashion, and in as false a manner as they could invent. But as the most cunning Charles celebrated one year the feast of the Birth and Coming of Christ at Trèves or Metz, and most carefully and cleverly grasped and understood the style of the singing; and then the next year passed the same solemn season at Paris or Tours, but found that the singing was wholly different from what he had heard in the preceding year; as moreover he found that those whom he had sent into different places were also at variance with one another; he reported the whole matter to Pope Leo, of holy memory, who had succeeded Stephen. The Pope summoned the clerks back to Rome and condemned them to exile or perpetual imprisonment, and then said to Charles: "If I send you others they will be blinded with the same malice as their predecessors and will not fail to cheat you. But I think I can satisfy your wishes in this way. Send me two of the cleverest clerks that you have by you, in such a way that those who are with me may not know that they belong to you, and, with God's help, they shall attain to as perfect a knowledge of those things as you desire." So said, so done. Soon the Pope sent them back excellently trained to Charles.

One of them he kept at his own court: the other upon the petition of his son Drogo, Bishop of Metz, he sent to that cathedral. And not only did his energy show itself powerful in that city, but it soon spread so widely throughout all Frankland, that now all in these regions who use the Latin tongue call the ecclesiastical chant Metensian; or, if they use the Teutonic or Teuthiscan tongue, they call it Mette; or if the Greek form is used it is called Mettisc. The most pious emperor also ordered Peter, the singer who had come to reside with him, to reside for a while in the monastery of St Gall. There too Charles established the chanting as it is to-day, with an authentic song-book, and gave most careful instructions, being always a warm champion of Saint Gall, that the Roman method of singing should be both taught and learnt. He gave to the monastery also much money and many lands: he gave too relics, contained in a reliquary made of solid gold and gems, which is called the Shrine of Charles.

11. It was the habit of the most religious and temperate Charles to take food during Lent at the seventh hour of the day after having been present at the celebration of mass and evening lauds: and in so doing he was not violating the fast for he was following the Lord's command in taking food at an

earlier hour than usual. Now a certain bishop, who offended against the precept of Solomon in being just but foolish, took him unwisely to task for this. Whereupon the most wise Charles concealed his wrath, and received the bishop's admonition in all humility, saying, "Good sir bishop, your admonition is good; and now my advice to you is that you should take no food until the very humblest of my servants, who stand in my court, have been fed." Now while Charles was eating he was waited upon by dukes and rulers and kings of various peoples; and when his banquet was ended then those who served him fed and they were served by counts and præfects and nobles of different ranks. And when these last had made an end of eating then came the military officers and the scholars of the palace: then the chiefs of the various departments of the palace; then their subordinates, then the servants of those servants. So that the last comers did not get a mouthful of food before the middle of the night. When therefore Lent was nearly ended, and the bishop in question had endured this punishment all the time, the most merciful Charles said to him: "Now, sir bishop, I think you have found out that it is not lack of self-restraint but care for others which makes me dine in Lent before the hour of evening."

L

Ↄ

12. Once he asked a bishop for his blessing and he thereupon, after blessing the bread, partook of it first himself and then wanted to give it to the most honourable Charles: who, however, said to him: "You may keep all the bread for yourself"; and much to the bishop's confusion he refused to receive his blessing.

13. The most careful Charles would never give more than one county to any of his counts unless they happened to live on the borders or marches of the barbarians; nor would he ever give a bishop any abbacy or church that was in the royal gift unless there were very special reasons for doing it. When his councillors or friends asked him the reason for this he would answer: "With that revenue or that estate, with that little abbey or that church I can secure the fidelity of some vassal, as good a man as any bishop or count, and perhaps better." But when there were special reasons he would give several benefices to one man; as he did for instance to Udalric, brother of the great Hildigard, the mother of kings and emperors. Now Udalric, after Hildigard's death, was deprived of his honours for a certain offence; and a buffoon thereupon said in the hearing of the most merciful Charles: "Now has Udalric, by the death of his sister, lost all his honours both

in east and west." Charles was touched by these words and restored to him at once all his former honours. He opened his hands, most widely and liberally, when justice bade him, to certain holy places, as will appear in the sequel.

14. There was a certain bishopric which lay full in Charles's path when he journeyed, and which indeed he could hardly avoid: and the bishop of this place, always anxious to give satisfaction, put everything that he had at Charles's disposal. But once the emperor came quite unexpectedly and the bishop in great anxiety had to fly hither and thither like a swallow, and had not only the palaces and houses but also the courts and squares swept and cleaned: and then, tired and irritated, came to meet him. The most pious Charles noticed this, and after examining all the various details, he said to the bishop: "My kind host, you always have everything splendidly cleaned for my arrival." Then the Bishop, as if divinely inspired, bowed his head and grasped the king's never-conquered right hand, and hiding his irritation, kissed it and said: "It is but right, my lord, that, wherever you come, all things should be thoroughly cleansed." Then Charles, of all kings the wisest, understanding the state of affairs said to him: "If I empty I can also fill." And

he added: "You may have that estate which lies close to your bishopric, and all your successors may have it until the end of time."

15. In the same journey too he came to a bishop who lived in a place through which he must needs pass. Now on that day, being the sixth day of the week, he was not willing to eat the flesh of beast or bird; and the bishop, being by reason of the nature of the place unable to procure fish upon the sudden, ordered some excellent cheese, rich and creamy, to be placed before him. And the most self-restrained Charles, with the readiness which he showed everywhere and on all occasions, spared the blushes of the bishop and required no better fare: but taking up his knife cut off the skin, which he thought unsavoury, and fell to on the white of the cheese. Thereupon the bishop, who was standing near like a servant, drew closer and said, "Why do you do that, lord emperor? You are throwing away the very best part." Then Charles, who deceived no one, and did not believe that anyone would deceive him, on the persuasion of the bishop put a piece of the skin in his mouth, and slowly ate it and swallowed it like butter. Then approving of the advice of the bishop, he said: "Very true, my good host," and he added: "Be sure to send me

every year to Aix two cart-loads of just such cheeses." The bishop was alarmed at the impossibility of the task and, fearful of losing both his rank and his office, he rejoined :—"My lord, I can procure the cheeses, but I cannot tell which are of this quality and which of another. Much I fear lest I fall under your censure." Then Charles from whose penetration and skill nothing could escape, however new or strange it might be, spoke thus to the bishop, who from childhood had known such cheeses and yet could not test them. "Cut them in two," he said, "then fasten together with a skewer those that you find to be of the right quality and keep them in your cellar for a time and then send them to me. The rest you may keep for yourself and your clergy and your family." This was done for two years and the king ordered the present of cheeses to be taken in without remark: then in the third year the bishop brought in person his laboriously collected cheeses. But the most just Charles pitied his labour and anxiety and added to the bishopric an excellent estate whence he and his successors might provide themselves with corn and wine.

16. As we have shown how the most wise Charles exalted the humble, let us now show how he brought low the proud. There was a bishop who sought

above measure vanities and the fame of men. The most cunning Charles heard of this and told a certain Jewish merchant, whose custom it was to go to the land of promise and bring from thence rare and wonderful things to the countries beyond the sea, to deceive or cheat this bishop in whatever way he could. So the Jew caught an ordinary household mouse and stuffed it with various spices, and then offered it for sale to the bishop, saying that he had brought this most precious never-before-seen animal from Judea. The bishop was delighted with what he thought a stroke of luck, and offered the Jew three pounds of silver for the precious ware. Then said the Jew, "A fine price indeed for so precious an article! I had rather throw it into the sea than let any man have it at so cheap and shameful a price." So the bishop, who had much wealth and never gave anything to the poor, offered him ten pounds of silver for the incomparable treasure. But the cunning rascal, with pretended indignation, replied: "The God of Abraham forbid that I should thus lose the fruit of my labour and journeyings." Then our avaricious bishop, all eager for the prize, offered twenty pounds. But the Jew in high dudgeon wrapped up the mouse in the most costly silk and made as if he would depart. Then the bishop, as thoroughly taken in as he deserved to be, offered a full measure of silver for the priceless object. And so at last our trader yielded to his entreaties with much show of reluctance: and, taking the money, went to the emperor and told him everything. A few days later the king called together all the bishops and chief men of the province to hold discourse with him; and, after many other matters had been considered, he ordered all that measure of silver to be brought and placed in the middle of the palace. Then thus he spoke and said:—"Fathers and guardians, bishops of our Church, you ought to minister to the poor, or rather to Christ in them, and not to seek after vanities. But now you act quite contrary to this; and are vainglorious and avaricious beyond all other men." Then he added: "One of you has given a Jew all this silver for a painted mouse." Then the bishop, who had been so wickedly deceived, threw himself at Charles's feet and begged pardon for his sin. Charles upbraided him in suitable words and then allowed him to depart in confusion.

17. This same bishop was left to take care of Hildigard, when the most warlike Charles was engaged in campaigns against the Huns. He was so puffed up by his intimacy with her that he had the audacity to ask her to allow him to use the golden sceptre of the incomparable Charles on festal days instead of his

episcopal staff. She deceived him cleverly, and said that she dare not give it to anyone, but that she would carry his request faithfully to the king. So, when Charles came back, she jestingly told him of the mad request of the bishop. He kindly promised to do what she wished and even more. So, when all Europe, so to speak, had come together to greet Charles after his victory over so mighty a people, he pronounced these words in the hearing of small and great : "Bishops should despise this world and inspire others by their example to seek after heavenly things. But now they are misled by ambition beyond all the rest of mankind ; and one of them not content with holding the first episcopal see in Germany has dared without my approval to claim my golden sceptre, which I carry to signify my royal will, in order that he might use it as his pastoral staff." The guilty man acknowledged his sin, received pardon and retired.

18. Now, my Lord Emperor Charles, I much fear that through my desire to obey your orders I may incur the enmity of all who have taken vows and especially of the highest clergy of all. But for all this I do not greatly care, if only I be not deprived of your protection.

Once that most religious Emperor Charles gave orders that all bishops throughout his wide domains should preach in the nave of their cathedral before a certain day, which he appointed, under penalty of being deprived of the episcopal dignity, if they failed to comply with the order.—But why do I say "dignity" when the apostle protests: "He that desires a bishopric desires a good work"? But in truth, most serene of kings, I must confess to you that there is great "dignity" in the office, but not the slightest "good work" is required. Well, the aforementioned bishop was at first alarmed at this command, because gluttony and pride were all his learning, and he feared that if he lost his bishopric he would lose at the same time his soft living. So he invited two of the chiefs of the palace on the festal day, and after the reading of the lesson mounted the pulpit as though he were going to address the people. All the people ran together in wonder at so unexpected an occurrence, except one poor red-headed fellow, who had his head covered with clouts, because he had no hat, and was foolishly ashamed of his red hair. Then the bishop —bishop in name but not in deed—called to his doorkeeper or rather his *scario* (whose dignity and duties went by the name of the ædileship among the ancient Romans) and said: "Bring me that man in the hat who is standing there near the door of the church." The doorkeeper made haste to obey, seized the poor man and began to drag him towards the bishop. But he feared some heavy penalty for daring to stand in the house of God with covered head, and struggled with all his might to avoid being brought before the tribunal of the terrible judge. But the bishop, looking from his perch, now addressing his vassals and now chiding the poor knave, bawled out and preached as follows:—"Here with him! don't let him slip! Willy-nilly you've got to come." When at last force or fear brought him near, the bishop cried: "Come forward; nay, you must come quite close." Then he snatched the head-covering from his captive and cried to the people:—"Lo and behold all ye people; the boor is red-headed." Then he returned to the altar and performed the ceremony, or pretended to perform it.

When the mass was thus scrambled through his guests passed into his hall, which was decorated with many-coloured carpets, and cloths of all kinds; and there a magnificent banquet, served in gold and silver and jewelled cups, was provided, calculated to tickle the appetite of the fastidious or the well-fed. The bishop himself sat on the softest of cushions, clad in precious silks and wearing the imperial purple, so that he seemed a king except for the sceptre and the title. He was surrounded by troops of rich knights, in comparison with whom the officers of the palace (nobles though they were) of the unconquered Charles seemed to themselves most mean. When they asked leave to depart after this wonderful and more than royal banquet he, desiring to show still more plainly his magnificence and his glory, ordered skilled musicians to come forward, the sound of whose voices could soften the hardest hearts or turn to ice the swiftly flowing waters of the Rhine. And at the same time every kind of choice drink, subtly and variously compounded, was offered them in bowls of gold and gems, whose sheen was mixed with that of the flowers and leaves with which they were crowned : but their stomachs could contain no more so that the glasses lay idle in their hands. Meanwhile pastry cooks and sausage makers, servers and dressers offered preparations of exquisite art to stimulate their appetite, though their stomachs could contain no more : it was a banquet such as was never offered even to the great Charles himself.

When morning came and the bishop returned some way towards soberness, he thought with fear of the luxury that he had paraded before the servants of the emperor. So he called them into his presence, loaded them with presents worthy of a king, and implored them to speak to the terrible Charles of the goodness and simplicity of his life ; and above all to tell him how he had preached publicly before them in his cathedral.

Upon their return Charles asked them why the bishop had invited them. Thereupon they fell at his feet and said : "Master, it was that he might honour us as your representatives, far beyond our humble deserts." "He is," they went on, "in every way the best and the most faithful of bishops and most worthy of the highest rank in the Church. For, if you will trust our poor judgment, we profess to your sublime majesty that we heard him preach in his church in the most stirring fashion." Then the emperor who knew the bishop's lack of skill pressed them further as to the manner of his preaching ; and they, perforce, revealed all. Then the emperor saw that he had made an effort to say something rather than disobey the imperial order ; and he allowed him, in spite of his unworthiness, to retain the bishopric.

19. Shortly after a young man, a relation of the emperor's, sang, on the occasion of some festival, the Allelulia admirably : and the Emperor turned to this same bishop and said : "My clerk is singing very well." But the stupid man, thought that he was jesting and did not know that the clerk was the

emperor's relation; and so he answered: "Any clown in our countryside drones as well as that to his oxen at their ploughing." At this vulgar answer the emperor turned on him the lightning of his flashing eyes and dashed him terror-stricken to the very ground.

26. But though the rest of mankind may be deceived by the wiles of the devil and his angels, it is pleasant to consider the word of our Lord, who in recognition of the bold confession of Saint Peter said:—"Thou art Peter, and upon this rock will I build my church; and the gates of hell shall not prevail against it." Wherefore even in these times of great peril and wickedness he has allowed the Church to remain unshaken and unmoved.

Now since envy always rages among the envious so it is customary and regular with the Romans to oppose or rather to fight against all strong Popes, who are from time to time raised to the apostolic see. Whence it came to pass that certain of the Romans, themselves blinded with envy, charged the above-mentioned Pope Leo of holy memory with a deadly crime and tried to blind him. But they were frightened and held back by some divine impulse, and after trying in vain to gouge out his eyes, they slashed them across the middle with knives. The Pope had news of this carried secretly by his servants to Michael, Emperor of Constantinople; but he refused all assistance saying: "The Pope has an independent kingdom and one higher than mine; so he must act his own revenge upon his enemies." Thereupon the holy Leo invited the unconquered Charles to come to Rome; following in this the ordinance of God, that, as Charles was already in very deed ruler and emperor over many nations, so also by the authority of the apostolic see he might have now the name of Emperor, Cæsar and Augustus. Now Charles, being always ready to march and in warlike array, though he knew nothing at all of the cause of the summons, came at once with his attendants and his vassals; himself the head of the world he came to the city that had once been the head of the world. And when the abandoned people heard of his sudden coming, at once, as sparrows hide themselves when they hear the voice of their master, so they fled and hid in various hiding-places, cellars, and dens. Nowhere however under heaven could they escape from his energy and penetration; and soon they were captured and brought in chains to the Cathedral of St Peter. Then the undaunted Father Leo took the gospel of our Lord Jesus Christ and held it over his head, and then in the presence of Charles and his knights, in presence also of his persecutors, he swore in the following words :—" So on the day of the great judgment may I partake in the promises, as I am innocent of the charge that is falsely laid against me." Then many of the prisoners asked to be allowed to swear upon the tomb of St Peter that they also were innocent of the charge laid against them. But the Pope knew their falseness and said to Charles : " Do not, I pray you, unconquered servant of God, give assent to their cûnning ; for well they know that Saint Peter is always ready to forgive. But seek among the tombs of the martyrs the stone upon which is written the name of St Pancras, that boy of thirteen years ; and if they will swear to you in his name you may know that you have them fast." It was done as the Pope ordered. And when many people drew near to take the oath upon this tomb, straightway some fell back dead and some were seized by the devil and went mad. Then the terrible Charles said to his servants : " Take care that none of them escapes." Then he condemned all who had been taken prisoner either to some kind of death or to perpetual imprisonment.

As Charles stayed in Rome for a few days, the bishop of the apostolic see called together all who would come from the neighbouring districts and then, in their presence and in the presence of all the knights of the unconquered Charles, he declared him to be Emperor and Defender of the Roman Church. Now Charles had no guess of what was coming; and, though he could not refuse what seemed to have been divinely preordained for him, nevertheless he received his new title with no show of thankfulness. For first he thought that the Greeks would be fired by greater envy than ever and would plan some harm against the kingdom of the Franks; or at least would take greater precautions against a possible sudden attack of Charles to subdue their kingdom, and add it to his own empire. And further the magnanimous Charles recalled how ambassadors from the King of Constantinople had come to him and had told him that their master wished to be his loyal friend; and that, if they became nearer neighbours, he had determined to treat him as his son and relieve the poverty of Charles from his resources: and how, upon hearing this, Charles was unable to contain any longer the fiery ardour of his heart and had exclaimed: "Oh, would that pool were not between us; for then we would either divide between us the wealth of the east, or we would hold it in common."

But the Lord, who is both the giver and the restorer of health, so showed his favour to the innocency of the blessed Leo that he restored his eyes to be brighter than they were before that wicked and cruel cutting; except only that, in token of his virtue, a bright scar (like a very fine thread) marked his eyelids.

27. The foolish may accuse me of folly because just now I made Charles say that the sea, which that mighty emperor called playfully a little pool, lay between us and the Greeks; but I must tell my critics that at that date the Bulgarians and the Huns and many other powerful races barred the way to Greece with forces yet unattacked and unbroken. Soon afterwards, it is true, the most warlike Charles either hurled them to the ground, as he did the Slavs and the Bulgars; or else utterly destroyed them, as was the case with the Huns, that race of iron and adamant. And I will go on to speak of these exploits as soon as I have given a very slight account of the wonderful buildings which Charles (Emperor, Augustus and Cæsar), following the example of the all-wise Solomon, built at Aix, either for God, or for himself, or for the bishops, abbots, counts and all guests that came to him from all quarters of the world.

28. When the most energetic Emperor Charles could rest awhile he sought not sluggish ease, but laboured in the service of God. He desired therefore to build upon his native soil a cathedral finer even than the works of the Romans, and soon his purpose was realised. For the building thereof he summoned architects and skilled workmen from all lands beyond the seas; and above all he placed a certain knavish abbot whose competence for the execution of such tasks he knew, though he knew not his character. When the august emperor had gone on a certain journey, this abbot allowed anyone to depart home who would pay sufficient money: and those who could not purchase their discharge, or were not allowed to return by their masters, he burdened with unending labours, as the Egyptians once afflicted the people of God. By such knavish tricks he gathered together a great mass of gold and silver and silken robes; and, exhibiting in his chamber only the least precious articles, he concealed in boxes and chests all the richest treasures. Well, one day there was brought to him on a sudden the news that his house was on fire. He ran, in great excitement, and pushed his way through the bursting flames into the strong room where his boxes, stuffed with gold, were kept: he was not satisfied to take

one away, but would only leave after he had loaded his servants with a box a piece. And as he was going out a huge beam, dislodged by the fire, fell on the top of him; and then his body was burnt by temporal and his soul by eternal flames. Thus did the judgment of God keep watch for the most religious Emperor Charles, when his attention was withdrawn by the business of his kingdom.

29. There was another workman, the most skilled of all in the working of brass and glass. Now this man (his name was Tancho and he was at one time a monk of St Gall) made a fine bell and the emperor was delighted with its tone. Then said that most distinguished, but most unfortunate worker in brass: "Lord emperor, give orders that a great weight of copper be brought to me that I may refine it; and instead of tin give me as much silver as I shall need—a hundred pounds at least; and I will cast such a bell for you that this will seem dumb in comparison to it." Then Charles, the most liberal of monarchs, who "if riches abounded set not his heart upon them" readily gave the necessary orders, to the great delight of the knavish monk. He smelted and refined the brass; but he used, not silver, but the purest sort of tin, and soon he made a bell, much better than the one that the emperor had formerly admired,

and, when he had tested it, he took it to the emperor, who admired its exquisite shape and ordered the clapper to be inserted and the bell to be hung in the bell-tower. That was soon done; and then the warden of the church, the attendants and even the boys of the place tried, one after the other, to make the bell sound. But all was in vain; and so at last the knavish maker of the bell came up, seized the rope, and pulled at the bell. When, lo and behold! down from on high came the brazen mass; fell on the very head of the cheating brass-founder; killed him on the spot; and passed straight through his carcass and crashed to the ground carrying his bowels with it. When the aforementioned weight of silver was found, the most righteous Charles ordered it to be distributed among the poorest servants of the palace.

30. Now it was a rule at that time that if the imperial mandate had gone out that any task was to be accomplished, whether it was the making of bridges, or ships or causeways, or the cleansing or paving or filling up of muddy roads, the counts might execute the less important work by the agency of their deputies or servants; but for the greater enterprises, and especially such as were of an original kind, no duke or count, no bishop or abbot could possibly

get himself excused. The arches of the great bridge at Mainz bear witness to this ; for all Europe, so to speak, laboured at this work in orderly co-operation, and then the knavery of a few rascals, who wanted to steal merchandise from the ships that passed underneath, destroyed it.

If any churches, within the royal domain, wanted decorating with carved ceilings or wall paintings, the neighbouring bishops and abbots had to take charge of the task ; but if new churches had to be built then all bishops, dukes and counts, all abbots and heads of royal churches and all who were in occupation of any public office had to work at it with never-ceasing labour from its foundations to its roof. You may see the proof of the emperor's skill in the cathedral at Aix, which seems a work half human and half divine ; you may see it in the mansions of the various dignitaries which, by Charles's device, were built round his own palace in such a way that from the windows of his chamber he could see all who went out or came in, and what they were doing, while they believed themselves free from observation ; you may see it in all the houses of his nobles, which were lifted on high from the ground in such a fashion that beneath them the retainers of his nobles and the servants of those retainers and every class of man could be protected from rain or snow, from cold or heat, while at the same time they were not concealed from the eyes of the most vigilant Charles. But I am a prisoner within my monastery walls and your ministers are free; and I will therefore leave to them the task of describing the cathedral, while I return to speak of how the judgment of God was made manifest in the building of it.

31. The most careful Charles ordered certain nobles of the neighbourhood to support with all their power the workmen whom he had set to their task, and to supply everything that they required for it. Those workmen who came from a distance he gave in charge to a certain Liutfrid, the steward of his palace, telling him to feed and clothe them and also most carefully to provide anything that was wanting for the building. The steward obeyed these commands for the short time that Charles remained in that place; but after his departure neglected them altogether, and by cruel tortures collected such a mass of money from the poor workmen that Dis and Pluto would require a camel to carry his ill-gotten gains to hell. Now this was found out in the following way.

The most glorious Charles used to go to lauds at night in a long and flowing cloak, which is now neither used nor known: then when the morning chant was over he would go back to his chamber and dress himself in his imperial robes. All the clerks used to come ready dressed to the nightly office, and then they would wait for the emperor's arrival, and for the celebration of mass either in the church or in the porch which then was called the outer court. Sometimes they would remain awake, or if anyone had need of sleep he would lean his head on his companion's breast. Now one poor clerk, who used often to go to Liutfrid's house to get his clothes (rags I ought to call them) washed and mended, was sleeping with his head on a friend's knees, when he saw in a vision a giant, taller than the adversary of Saint Anthony, come from the king's court and hurry over the bridge, that spanned a little stream, to the house of the steward; and he led with him an enormous camel, burdened with baggage of inestimable value. He was, in his dream, struck with amazement and he asked the giant who he was and whither he wished to go. And the giant made answer: "I come from the house of the king and I go to the house of Liutfrid; and I shall place Liutfrid on these packages and I shall take him and them down with me to hell."

Thereupon the clerk woke up, in a fright lest Charles should find him sleeping. He lifted up his head and urged the others to wakefulness and cried: "Hear, I pray you, my dream. I seemed to see another Polyphemus, who walked on the earth and yet touched the stars, and passed through the Ionian Sea without wetting his sides. I saw him hasten from the royal court to the house of Liutfrid with a laden camel. And when I asked the cause of his journey, he said: 'I am going to put Liutfrid on the top of the load, and then take him to hell.'"

The story was hardly finished when there came from that house, which they all knew so well, a girl who fell at their feet and asked them to remember her friend Liutfrid in their prayers. And, when they asked the reason for her words, she said: "My lord, he went out but now in good health, and, as he stayed a long time, we went in search of him, and found him dead."

When the emperor heard of his sudden death, and was informed by the workmen and his servants of his grasping avarice, he ordered his treasures to be examined. They were found to be of priceless worth, and when the emperor, after God the greatest of judges, found by what wickedness they had been collected he gave this public judgment: "Nothing of that which was gained by fraud must go to the liberation of his soul from purgatory. Let his wealth be divided among the workmen of this our building, and the poorer servants of our palace."

32. Now I must speak of two things which happened in that same place. There was a deacon who followed the Italian custom and resisted the course of nature. For he went to the baths and had himself closely shaved, polished his skin, cleaned his nails, and had his hair cut as short as if it had been done by a lathe. Then he put on linen and a white robe, and then, because he must not miss his turn, or rather desiring to make a fine show, he proceeded to read the gospel before God and His holy angels, and in presence of the most watchful king; his heart in the meantime being unclean, as events were to show. For while he was reading, a spider came down from the ceiling by a thread, hooked itself on to the deacon's head, and then ran up again. The most observant Charles saw this happen a second and a third time, but pretended not to notice it, and the clerk, because of the emperor's presence, dare not keep off the spider with his hand, and moreover did not know that it was a spider attacking him, but thought that it was merely the tickling of a fly. So he finished the reading of the gospel, and also went through the rest of the office. But when he left the cathedral he soon began to swell up, and

died within an hour. But the most scrupulous Charles, inasmuch as he had seen his danger and had not prevented it, thought himself guilty of manslaughter and did public penance.

33. Now the most glorious Charles had in his suite a certain clerk who was unsurpassed in every respect. And of him that was said which was never said of any other mortal man : for it was said that he excelled all mankind in knowledge of both sacred and profane literature ; in song whether ecclesiastical or festive; in the composition and rendering of poems and in the sweet fulness of his voice and in the incredible pleasure which he gave. [Other men have had drawbacks to compensate for their excellences] : for Moses, the lawgiver filled with wisdom by the teaching of God, complains nevertheless that "he is not eloquent" but slow of speech, and "of a slow tongue," and sent therefore Joshua to take counsel with Eleasar, the high priest, who by the authority of the God, who dwelt within him, commanded even the heavenly bodies : and our Master Christ did not allow John the Baptist to work any miracle while in the body, though he bare witness that "among them that are born of women there hath not arisen a greater" than he : and He bade Peter revere the wisdom of Paul, though Peter

by the revelation of the Father recognised Him and received from Him the keys of the kingdom of heaven : and He allowed John His best-loved disciple to fall into so great a terror that he did not dare to come to the place of His sepulchre, though weak women paid many visits to it.

But as the scriptures say : "To him that hath shall be given" ; and those, who know from whom they have the little which they possess, succeed ; while he who knows not the giver of his possessions, or, if he knows it, gives not due thanks to the Giver, loses all. For, while this wonderful clerk was standing in friendly fashion near the most glorious emperor, suddenly he disappeared. The unconquered Emperor Charles was dumfoundered at so unheard of and incredible an occurrence : but, after he had made the sign of the cross, he found in the place where the clerk had stood something that seemed to be a foul-smelling coal, which had just ceased to burn.

34. The mention of the trailing garment that the emperor wore at night has diverted us from his military array. Now the dress and equipment of the old Franks was as follows :—Their boots were gilt on the outside and decorated with laces three cubits long. The thongs round the legs were red, and under them they wore upon their legs and thighs

linen of the same colour, artistically embroidered. The laces stretched above these linen garments and above the crossed thongs, sometimes under them and sometimes over them, now in front of the leg and now behind. Then came a rich linen shirt and then a buckled sword-belt. The great sword was surrounded first with a sheath, then with a covering of leather, and lastly with a linen wrap hardened with shining wax.

The last part of their dress was a white or blue cloak in the shape of a double square ; so that when it was placed upon the shoulders it touched the feet in front and behind, but at the side hardly came down to the knees. In the right hand was carried a stick of apple-wood, with regular knots, strong and terrible ; a handle of gold or silver decorated with figures was fastened to it. I myself am lazy and slower than a tortoise, and so never got into Frankland ; but I saw the King of the Franks in the monastery of Saint Gall, glittering in the dress that I have described.

But the habits of man change ; and when the Franks, in their wars with the Gauls, saw the latter proudly wearing little striped cloaks, they dropped their national customs and began to imitate the Gauls. At first the strictest of emperors did not forbid the new habit, because it seemed more suitable for war : but, when he found that the Frisians were abusing his permission, and were selling these little cloaks at the same price as the old large ones, he gave orders that no one should buy from them, at the usual price, anything but the old cloaks, broad, wide and long: and he added: "What is the good of those little napkins? I cannot cover myself with them in bed and when I am on horseback I cannot shield myself with them against wind and rain."

In the preface to this little work I said I would follow three authorities only. But as the chief of these, Werinbert, died seven days ago and to-day (the thirteenth of May) we, his bereaved sons and disciples, are going to pay solemn honour to his memory, here I will bring this book to an end, concerning the piety of Lord Charles and his care of the Church, which has been taken from the lips of this same clerk, Werinbert.

The next book which deals with the wars of the most fierce Charles is founded on the narrative of Werinbert's father, Adalbert. He followed his master Kerold in the Hunnish, Saxon and Slavic wars, and when I was quite a child, and he a very old man, I lived in his house and he used often to tell me the story of these events. I was most unwilling to listen and would often run away; but in the end by sheer force he made me hear.

BOOK II

CONCERNING THE WARS AND MILITARY EXPLOITS OF CHARLES

As I am going to found this narrative on the story told by a man of the world, who had little skill in letters, I think it will be well that I should first recount something of earlier history on the credit of written books. When Julian, whom God hated, was slain in the Persian war by a blow from heaven, not only did the transmarine provinces fall away from the Roman Empire, but also the neighbouring provinces of Pannonia, Noricum, Rhætia, or in other words the Germans and the Franks or Gauls. Then too the kings of the Franks (or Gauls) began to decay in power because they had slain Saint Didier, Bishop of Vienna, and had expelled those most holy visitors, Columban and Gall. Whereupon the race of the Huns, who had already often ravaged Francia and Aquitania (that is to say the Gauls and the Spains), now poured out with all their forces, devastated the whole land like a wide-sweeping conflagration, and then carried off all their spoils to a very safe hiding-place. Now Adalbert, whom I have already mentioned, used to explain the nature of this hiding-place as follows :—"The land of the Huns," he would say, "was surrounded by nine rings." I could not think of any rings except our ordinary wicker rings for sheepfolds ; and so I asked : "What, in the name of wonder, do you mean, sire?" "Well," he said, "it was fortified by nine hedges." I could not think of any hedges except those that protect our cornfields, so again I asked and he answered : "One ring was as wide, that is, it contained as much within it, as all the country between Tours and Constance. It was fashioned with logs of oak and ash and yew and was twenty feet wide and the same in height. All the space within was filled with hard stones and binding clay ; and the surface of these great ramparts was covered with sods and grass. Within the limits of the ring shrubs were planted of such a kind that, when lopped and bent down, they still threw out twigs and leaves. Then between these ramparts hamlets and houses were so arranged that a man's voice could be made to reach from one to the other. And opposite to the houses, at intervals in those unconquerable walls, were constructed doors of no great size; and through these doors the inhabitants from far and near would pour out on marauding expeditions. The second ring was like the first and was distant twenty Teutonic miles (or forty Italian) from the third ring: and so on to the ninth: though of course the successive rings were each much narrower than the preceding one. But in all the circles the estates and houses were everywhere so arranged that the peal of the trumpet would carry the news of any event from one to the other."

For two hundred years and more the Huns had swept the wealth of the western states within these fortifications, and as the Goths and Vandals were disturbing the repose of the world at the same time the western world was almost turned into a desert. But the most unconquerable Charles so subdued them in eight years that he allowed scarcely any traces of them to remain. He withdrew his hand from the Bulgarians, because after the destruction of the Huns they did not seem likely to do any harm to the kingdom of the Franks. All the booty of the Huns, which he found in Pannonia, he divided most liberally among the bishoprics and the monasteries.

2. In the Saxon war in which he was engaged in person for some considerable time, two private men (whose names I know, but modesty forbids me to give them) organised a storming party, and destroyed with great courage the walls of a very strong city and fortification. When the most just Charles saw this he made one of them, with the consent of his master Kerold, commander of the country between the Rhine and the Italian Alps and the other he enriched with gifts of land.

3. At the same time there were the sons of two nobles whose duty it was to watch at the door of the king's tent. But one night they lay as dead, soaked in liquor; while Charles, wakeful as usual, went the round of the camp, and came back to his tent without anyone having noticed him. When morning came he called to him the chiefs of his kingdom, and asked them what punishment seemed due to those who betrayed the King of the Franks into the hands ot the enemy. Then these nobles, quite ignorant of what had occurred, declared that such a man was worthy of death. But Charles merely upbraided them bitterly and let them go unharmed.

4. There were also with him two bastards, the

children of a concubine. As they had fought in battle most bravely, the emperor asked them whose children they were, and where they were born. When he was informed of the facts, he called them to his tent at midday and said: "My good fellows, I want you to serve me, and me only." They exclaimed that they were there for no other purpose than to take even the lowest place in his service. "Well then," said Charles, "you must serve in my chamber." They concealed their indignation and said they would be glad to do so; but soon they seized the moment when the emperor had begun to sleep soundly, and then rushed out to the camp of the enemy and, in the fray that followed, wiped out the taint of servitude in their own blood and that of the enemy.

5. But occupations such as these did not prevent the high-souled emperor from sending frequent messengers, carrying letters and presents, to the kings of the most distant regions; and they sent him in turn whatever honours their lands could bestow. From the theatre of the Saxon war he sent messengers to the King of Constantinople; who asked them whether the kingdom of "his son Charles" was at peace or was being invaded by the neighbouring peoples. Then the leader of the embassy made answer that

peace reigned everywhere, except only that a certain race called the Saxons were disturbing the territories of the Franks by frequent raids. Whereupon the sluggish and unwarlike Greek king answered: "Pooh! why should my son take so much trouble about a petty enemy that possesses neither fame nor valour? I will give you the Saxon race and all that belong to it." When the envoy on his return gave this message to the most warlike Charles, he smiled and said: "The king would have shown greater kindness to you if he had given you a leg-wrap for your long journey."

6. I must not conceal the wise answer which the same envoy gave during his embassy to Greece. He came with his companions to one of the royal towns in the autumn; the party was divided for entertainment, and the envoy of whom I speak was quartered on a certain bishop. This bishop was given up to fasting and prayer, and left the envoy to perish of almost continuous hunger: but, with the first smile of spring, he presented the envoy to the king. The king asked him his opinion of the bishop. Then the envoy sighed from the very bottom of his heart and said: "That bishop of yours reaches the highest point of holiness that can be attained to without God." The king was amazed,

and said: "What! can a man be holy without God?" Then said the envoy: "It is written, 'God is love,' and in that grace he is entirely lacking."

Thereupon the King of Constantinople invited him to his banquet and placed him among his nobles. Now these had a law that no guest at the king's table, whether a native or a foreigner, should turn over any animal or part of an animal: he must eat only the upper part of whatever was placed before him. Now, a river fish, covered with spice, was brought and placed on the dish before him. He knew nothing of the custom and turned the fish over whereupon all the nobles rose up and cried: "Master, you are dishonoured, as no king ever was before you." Then the king groaned and said to our envoy: "I cannot resist them: you must be put to death at once: but ask me any other favour you like and I will grant it." He thought awhile and then in the hearing of all pronounced these words: "I pray you, lord emperor, that in accordance with your promise you will grant me one small petition." And the king said: "Ask what you will, and you shall have it: except only that I may not give you your life, for that is against the law of the Greeks." Then said the envoy: "With my dying breath I ask one favour; let everyone who saw me turn that fish over be deprived of his eyes." The king was amazed at the stipulation, and swore, by Christ, that he had seen nothing, but had only trusted the word of others. Then the queen began to excuse herself: "By the beneficent Mother of God, the Holy Mary, I noticed nothing." Then the other nobles, in their desire to escape from the danger, swore, one by the keeper of the keys of heaven, and another by the apostle of the Gentiles, and all the rest by the virtue of the angels and the companies of the saints, that they were beyond the reach of the stipulation. And so the clever Frank beat the empty-headed Greeks in their own land and came home safe and sound.

A few years later the unwearied Charles sent to Greece a certain bishop remarkable both for his physical and mental gifts, and with him the most noble Duke Hugo. After a long delay they were at last brought into the presence of the king and then sent about to all manner of places. But at last they got their dismissal and returned, after paying heavily for their journey by sea and land.

Soon afterwards the Greek king sent his envoy to the most glorious Charles. It so happened that the bishop and the duke whom I have mentioned were just then with the emperor. When it was announced that the envoys were coming they advised the most wise Charles to have them led round through mountains and deserts, so that they should only come into the emperor's presence when their clothes had been worn and wasted, and their money was entirely spent.

This was done ; and, when at last they arrived, the bishop and his comrade bade the count of the stables take his seat on a high throne in the midst of his underlings, so that it was impossible to believe him anyone lower than the emperor. When the envoys saw him they fell upon the ground and wanted to worship him. But they were prevented by the ministers and forced to go farther. Then they saw the count of the palace presiding over a gathering of the nobles and again they thought it was the emperor and flung themselves to earth. But those who were present drove them forward with blows and said : "That is not the emperor." Next they saw the master of the royal table surrounded by his noble band of servants ; and again they fell to the ground thinking that it was the emperor. Driven thence they found the chamberlains of the emperor and their chief in council together ; and then they did not doubt but that they were in the presence of the first of living men. But this man too denied that he was what they took him for ; and yet he promised that he would use his influence with the nobles of the palace, so that if possible the envoys might come into the presence of the most august emperor. Then there came servants from the imperial presence to introduce them with full honours. Now Charles, the most gracious of kings, was standing by an open window leaning upon Bishop Heitto, for that was the name of the bishop who had been sent to Constantinople. The emperor was clad in gems and gold and glittered like the sun at its rising: and round about him stood, as it were the chivalry of heaven, three young men, his sons, who have since been made partners in the kingdom; his daughters and their mother decorated with wisdom and beauty as well as with pearls; leaders of the Church, unsurpassed in dignity and virtue; abbots distinguished for their high birth and their sanctity; nobles, like Joshua when he appeared in the camp of Gilgal; and an army like that which drove back the Syrians and Assyrians out of Samaria. So that if David had been there he might well have sung: "Kings of the earth and all people; princes and all judges of the earth; both young men and maidens; old men and children let them praise the name of the Lord." Then the envoys of the Greeks were astonished; their spirit left them and their courage failed;

speechless and lifeless they fell upon the ground. But the most kindly emperor raised them, and tried to cheer them with encouraging words. At last life returned to them; but when they saw Heitto, whom they had once despised and rejected, now in so great honour, again they grovelled on the ground in terror; until the king swore to them by the King of Heaven that he would do them no harm. They took heart at this promise and began to act with a little more confidence; and so home they went and never came back again.

7. And here I must repeat that the most illustrious Charles had men of the greatest cleverness in all offices. When the morning lauds had been celebrated before the emperor on the octave of the Epiphany, the Greeks proceeded privately to sing to God in their own language psalms with the same melody and the same subject matter as "*Veterem hominem*" and the following words in our missal. Thereupon the emperor ordered one of his chaplains, who understood the Greek tongue, to adopt that psalm in Latin to the same melody, and to take special care that a separate syllable corresponded to every separate note, so that the Latin and Greek should resemble one another as far as the nature of the two languages allowed. So it came to pass

that all of them have been written in the same rhythm, and in one of them *conteruit* has been substituted for "*contrivit.*"

These same Greek envoys brought with them every kind of organ, as well as other instruments of various kinds. All of these were covertly inspected by the workmen of the most wise Charles, and then exactly reproduced. The chief of these was that musicians' organ, wherein the great chests were made of brass: and bellows of ox-hide blew through pipes of brass, and the bass was like the roaring of the thunder, and in sweetness it equalled the tinkling of lyre or cymbal. But I must not, here and now, speak of where it was set up, and how long it lasted, and how it perished at the same time as other losses fell upon the state.

8. About the same time also envoys of the Persians were sent to him. They knew not where Frankland lay; but because of the fame of Rome, over which they knew that Charles had rule, they thought it a great thing when they were able to reach the coast of Italy. They explained the reason of their journey to the Bishops of Campania and Tuscany, of Emilia and Liguria, of Burgundy and Gaul and to the abbots and counts of those regions; but by all they were either deceitfully handled or else

actually driven off; so that a whole year had gone round before, weary and footsore with their long journey, they reached Aix at last and saw Charles, the most renowned of kings by reason of his virtues. They arrived in the last week of Lent, and, on their arrival being made known to the emperor, he postponed their presentation until Easter Eve. Then when that incomparable monarch was dressed with incomparable magnificence for the chief of festivals, he ordered the introduction of the envoys of that race that had once held the whole world in awe. But they were so terrified at the sight of the most magnificent Charles that one might think they had never seen king or emperor before. He received them however most kindly, and granted them this privilege—that they might go wherever they had a mind to, even as one of his own children, and examine everything and ask what questions and make what inquiries they chose. They jumped with joy at this favour, and valued the privilege of clinging close to Charles, of gazing upon him, of admiring him, more than all the wealth of the east.

They went up into the ambulatory that runs round the nave of the cathedral and looked down upon the clergy and the nobles; then they returned to the emperor, and, by reason of the greatness of their joy, they could not refrain from laughing aloud; and they clapped their hands and said:— "We have seen only men of clay before: here are men of gold." Then they went to the nobles, one by one, and gazed with wonder upon arms and clothes that were strange to them; and then came back to the emperor, whom they regarded with wonder still greater. They passed that night and the next Sunday continuously in church; and, upon the most holy day itself, they were invited by the most munificent Charles to a splendid banquet, along with the nobles of Frankland and Europe. There they were so struck with amazement at the strangeness of everything that they had hardly eaten anything at the end of the banquet.

"But when the Morn, leaving Tithonus' bed,
Illumined all the land with Phœbus' torch"

then Charles, who would never endure idleness and sloth, went out to the woods to hunt the bison and the urochs; and made preparations to take the Persian envoys with him. But when they saw the immense animals they were stricken with a mighty fear and turned and fled. But the undaunted hero

Charles, riding on a high-mettled charger, drew near to one of these animals and drawing his sword tried to cut through its neck. But he missed his aim, and the monstrous beast ripped the boot and leg-thongs of the emperor; and, slightly wounding his calf with the tip of its horn, made him limp slightly: after that, furious at the failure of its stroke, it fled to the shelter of a valley, which was thickly covered with stones and trees. Nearly all his servants wanted to take off their own hose to give to Charles, but he forbade it saying: "I mean to go in this fashion to Hildigard." Then Isambard, the son of Warin (the same Warin that persecuted your patron Saint Othmar), ran after the beast and not daring to approach him more closely, threw his lance and pierced him to the heart between the shoulder and the wind-pipe, and brought the beast yet warm to the emperor. He seemed to pay no attention to the incident; but gave the carcass to his companions and went home. But then he called the queen and showed her how his leg-coverings were torn, and said: "What does the man deserve who freed me from the enemy that did this to me?" She made answer: "He deserves the highest boon." Then the emperor told the whole story and produced the enormous horns of the beast in witness of his truth: so that the empress sighed and wept and beat her breast. But when she heard that it was Isambard, who had saved him from this terrible enemy, Isambard, who was in ill favour with the emperor and who had been deprived of all his offices—she threw herself at his feet and induced him to restore all that had been taken from him; and a largess was given to him besides.

These same Persian envoys brought the emperor an elephant, monkeys, balsam, nard, unguents of various kinds, spices, scents and many kinds of drugs: in such profusion that it seemed as if the east had been left bare that the west might be filled. They came by-and-by to stand on very familiar terms with the emperor; and one day, when they were in a specially merry mood and a little heated with strong beer, they spoke in jest as follows:—"Sir emperor, your power is indeed great; but much less than the report of it which is spread through all the kingdoms of the east." When he heard this he concealed his deep displeasure and asked jestingly of them: "Why do you say that, my children? How did that idea get into your heads?" Then they went back to the beginning and told him everything that had happened to them in the lands beyond the sea; and they said:—"We Persians and the Medes, Armenians, Indians, Parthians, Elamites, and all the inhabitants of the east fear you much more than our own ruler Haroun. And the Macedonians and all the Greeks (how shall we express it?) they are beginning to fear your overwhelming greatness more than the waves of the Ionian Sea. And the inhabitants of all the islands through which we passed were as ready to obey you, and as much devoted to your service, as if they had been reared in your palace and loaded with your favours. But the nobles of your own kingdom, it seems to us, care very little about you except in your presence: for when we came as strangers to them, and begged them to show us some kindness for the love of you, to whom we desired to make our way, they gave no heed to us and sent us away empty-handed." Then the emperor deposed all counts and abbots, through whose territories those envoys had come, from all the offices that they held; and fined the bishops in a huge sum of money. Then he ordered the envoys to be taken back to their own country with all care and honour.

9. There came to him also envoys from the King of the Africans, bringing a Marmorian lion and a Numidian bear, with Spanish iron and Tyrian

purple, and other noteworthy products of those regions. The most munificent Charles knew that the king and all the inhabitants of Africa were oppressed by constant poverty; and so, not only on this occasion but all through his life, he made them presents of the wealth of Europe, corn and wine and oil, and gave them liberal support; and thus he kept them constantly loyal and obedient to himself, and received from them a considerable tribute.

Soon after the unwearied emperor sent to the emperor of the Persians horses and mules from Spain; Frisian robes, white, grey, red and blue; which in Persia, he was told, were rarely seen and highly prized. Dogs too he sent him of remarkable swiftness and fierceness, such as the King of Persia had desired, for the hunting and catching of lions and tigers. The King of Persia cast a careless eye over the other presents, but asked the envoys what wild beasts or animals these dogs were accustomed to fight with. He was told that they would pull down quickly anything they were set on to. "Well," he said, "experience will test that." Next day the shepherds were heard crying loudly as they fled from a lion. When the noise came to the palace of the king, he said to the envoys: "Now, my friends of Frankland, mount your horses and follow me." Then they eagerly followed after the king as though they had never known toil or weariness. When they came in sight of the lion, though he was yet at a distance, the satrap of the satraps said to them: "Now set your dogs on to the lion." They obeyed and eagerly galloped forward; the German dogs caught the Persian lion, and the envoys slew him with swords of northern metal, which had already been tempered in the blood of the Saxons.

At this sight Haroun, the bravest inheritor of that name, understood the superior might of Charles from very small indications, and thus broke out in his praise:—"Now I know that what I heard of my brother Charles is true: how that by the frequent practice of hunting, and by the unwearied training of his body and mind, he has acquired the habit of subduing all that is beneath the heavens. How can I make worthy recompense for the honours which he has bestowed upon me? If I give him the land which was promised to Abraham and shown to Joshua, it is so far away that he could not defend it from the barbarians: or if, like the high-souled king that he is, he tried to defend it I fear that the provinces which lie upon the frontiers of the Frankish kingdom would revolt from his empire. But in this way I will try to show my gratitude for his generosity. I will give that land into his power; and I will rule over it as his representative. Whenever he likes or whenever there is a good opportunity he shall send me envoys; and he will find me a faithful manager of the revenue of that province."

Thus was brought to pass what the poet spoke of as an impossibility:—

"The Parthian's eyes the Arar's stream shall greet
And Tigris' waves shall lave the German's feet":

for through the energy of the most vigorous Charles it was found not merely possible but quite easy for his envoys to go and return; and the messengers of Haroun, whether young or old, passed easily from Parthia into Germany and returned from Germany to Parthia. (And the poet's words are true, whatever interpretation the grammarians put on "the river Arar," whether they think it an affluent of the Rhone or the Rhine; for they have fallen into confusion on this point through their ignorance of the locality). I could call on Germany to bear witness to my words; for in the time of your glorious father Lewis the land was compelled to pay a penny for every acre of land held under the law towards the redemption of Christian captives in the Holy Land; and they made their wretched appeal in the name of the dominion anciently held over that land by your great-grandfather Charles and your grandfather Lewis.

10. Now as the occasion has arisen to make honourable mention of your never-sufficiently-praised father, I should like to recall some prophetic words which the most wise Charles is known to have uttered about him. When he was six years old and had been most carefully reared in the house of his father, he was thought (and justly) to be wiser than men sixty years of age. His father then, hardly thinking it possible that he could bring him to see his grandfather, nevertheless took him from his mother, who had reared him with the most tender care, and began to instruct him how to conduct himself with propriety and modesty in the presence of the emperor; and how if he were asked a question he was to make answer and show in all things deference to his father. Thereafter he took him to the palace; and, on the first or second day, the emperor noted him with interest standing among the rest of the courtiers. "Who is that little fellow?" he said to his son; and he had for answer: "He is mine, sire; and yours if you deign to have him." So he said: "Give him to

me" ; and, when that was done, he took the little fellow and kissed him and sent him back to the place where he had formerly stood. But now he knew his own rank ; and thought it shame to stand lower than any one who was lower in rank than the emperor ; so with perfect composure of mind and body he took his place on terms of equality with his father. The most prophetic Charles noticed this ; and, calling his son Lewis, told him to find out the name of the boy ; and why he acted in this way ; and what it was that made him bold enough to claim equality with his father. The answer that Lewis got was founded on good reason : "When I was your vassal," he said, "I stood behind you and among soldiers of my own rank, as I was bound to do : but now I am your ally and comrade in arms, and so I rightly claim equality with you." When Lewis reported this to the emperor, the latter gave utterance to words something like these :—"If that little fellow lives he will be something great." (I have borrowed these words from the Life of Saint Ambrose, because the actual words that Charles used cannot be translated directly into Latin. And it seems fair to apply the prophecy which was made of Saint Ambrose to Lewis ; for Lewis closely resembled the saint, except in such points as are necessary to an earthly commonwealth, as for instance marriage and the use of arms; and in the power of his kingdom and his zeal for religion, Lewis was, if I may say so, superior to Saint Ambrose. He was a Catholic in faith, devoted to the worship of God, and the unwearied ally, protector, and defender of the servants of Christ.

Here is an instance of this. When our faithful Abbot Hartmuth—who is now your hermit—reported to him that the little endowment of Saint Gall, which was due not to royal munificence but to the petty offerings of private people, was not defended by any special charter such as other monasteries have, nor even by the laws that are common to all people, and so was unable to procure any defender or advocate, King Lewis himself resisted all our opponents, and was not ashamed to proclaim himself the champion of our weakness in the presence of all his nobles. At the same time too he wrote a letter to your genius directing that we should have licence to make petition, after taking a special vote, for whatever we would through your authority. But alas, what a stupid creature I am! I have been probably drawn aside by my personal gratitude for the special kindness he showed us, away from his general and indescribable goodness and greatness and nobleness.)

11. Now Lewis, King and Emperor of all Germany, of the provinces of Rhætia and of ancient Francia, of Saxony too and of Thuringia, of the provinces of Pannonia and of all northern nations, was of large build and handsome; his eyes sparkled like the stars, his voice was clear and manly. His wisdom was quite out of the common, and he added to it by constantly applying his singularly acute intellect to the study of the scriptures. He showed wonderful quickness too in anticipating or overcoming the plots of his enemies, in bringing to an end the quarrels of his subjects, and in procuring every kind of advantage for those who were loyal to him. More even than his ancestors he came to be a terror to all the heathen that stood round about his kingdom. And he deserved his good fortune; for he never defiled his tongue by condemning, nor his hands by shedding Christian blood: except once only, and then upon the most absolute necessity. But I dare not tell that story until I see a little Lewis or a Charles standing by your side. After that one slaughter, nothing could induce him to condemn anyone to death. But the measure of compulsion which he used against those who were accused of disloyalty or plots was merely this: he deprived them of office, and no new circumstance

and no length of time could then soften his heart so as to restore them to the former rank. He surpassed all men in his zealous devotion to prayer, religious fasting and the care of the service of God; and like Saint Martin, whatever he was doing, he prayed to God as though he were face to face with Him. On certain days he abstained from flesh and all pleasant food. At the time of litanies he used to follow the cross with unshod feet from his palace as far as the cathedral; or if he were at Regensburg as far as the church of Saint Hemmeramm. In other places he followed the customs of those whom he was with. He built new oratories of wonderful workmanship at Frankfurt and Regensburg. In the latter place, as stones were wanting to complete the immense fabric, he ordered the walls of the city to be pulled down; and in certain holes in the wall they found bones of men long dead, wrapped in so much gold, that not only did it serve to decorate the cathedral, but also he was able to furnish certain books that were written on the subject with cases of the same material nearly a finger thick. No clerk could stay with him, or even come into his presence, unless he were able to read and chant. He despised monks who broke their vows, and loved those who kept them. He was so full of sweet-tempered mirth, that, if anyone came to him in a morose mood, merely to see him and exchange a few words with him sent the visitor away with raised spirits. If anything evil or foolish was done in his presence, or if it happened that he were told of it, then a single glance of his eyes was enough to check everything, so that what is written of the eternal Judge who sees the hearts of men (viz. "A King that sitteth on the throne of judgment, scattereth away all evil with His eyes") might be fairly said to have begun in him, beyond what is usually granted to mortals.

All this I have written by way of digression, hoping that, if life lasts and Heaven is propitious, I may in time to come write much more concerning him.

12. But I must return to my subject. While Charles was detained for a little at Aix by the arrival of many visitors and the hostility of the unconquered Saxons and the robbery and piracy of the Northmen and Moors, and while the war against the Huns was being conducted by his son Pippin, the barbarous nations of the north attacked Noricum and eastern Frankland and ravaged a great part of it. When he heard of this he humiliated them in his own person; and he gave orders that all the boys and children of the invaders should be "measured with the sword";

and if anyone exceeded that measurement he should be shortened by a head.

This incident led to another much greater and more important. For, when your imperial majesty's most holy grandfather departed from life, certain giants (like to those who, Scripture tells us, were begotten by the sons of Seth from the daughters of Cain), blown up with the spirit of pride and doubtless like to those who said, "What part have we in David and what inheritance in the son of Esau?"—these mighty men, I say, despised the most worthy children of Charles, and each tried to seize for himself the command in the kingdom and themselves to wear the crown. Then some of the middle class were moved by the inspiration of God to declare that, as the renowned Emperor Charles had once measured the enemies of Christianity with the sword, so, as long as any of his progeny could be found of the length of a sword, he must rule over the Franks and over all Germany too: thereupon that devilish group of conspirators was as it were struck with a thunderbolt, and scattered in all directions.

But, after conquering the external foe, Charles was attacked at the hands of his own people in a remarkable but unavailing plot. For on his return from the Slavs into his own kingdom he was nearly captured and put to death by his son, whom a concubine had borne to him and who had been called by his mother by the ill-omened name of the most glorious Pippin. The plot was found out in the following manner. This son of Charles had been plotting the death of the emperor with a gathering of nobles, in the church of Saint Peter ; and when their debate was over, fearful of every shadow, he ordered search to be made, to see whether anyone was hidden in the corners or under the altar. And behold they found, as they feared, a clerk hidden under the altar. They seized him and made him swear that he would not reveal their conspiracy. To save his life, he dared not refuse to take the oath which they dictated : but, when they were gone, he held his wicked oath of small account and at once hurried to the palace. With the greatest difficulty he passed through the seven bolted gates, and coming at length to the emperor's chamber knocked upon the door. The most vigilant Charles fell into a great astonishment, as to who it was that dared to disturb him at that time of night. He however ordered the women (who followed in his train to wait upon the queen and the princesses) to go out and see who was at the door and what he wanted. When they went out and found the wretched creature, they bolted the door in his face and then, bursting with laughter and stuffing their dresses into their mouths, they tried to hide themselves in the corners of the apartments. But that most wise emperor, whose notice nothing under heaven could escape, asked straitly of the women who it was and what he wanted. When he was told that it was a smooth-faced, silly, half-mad knave, dressed only in shirt and drawers, who demanded an audience without delay, Charles ordered him to be admitted. Then he fell at the emperor's feet and showed all that had happened. So all the conspirators, entirely unsuspicious of danger, were seized before the third hour of the day and most deservedly condemned to exile or some other form of punishment. Pippin himself, a dwarf and a hunchback, was cruelly scourged, tonsured, and sent for some time as a punishment to the monastery of Saint Gall; the poorest, it was judged, and the straitest in all the emperor's broad dominions.

A short time afterwards some of the Frankish nobles sought to do violence to their king. Charles was well aware of their intentions, and yet did not wish to destroy them; because, if only they were loyal, they might be a great protection to all Christian men. So he sent messengers to this Pippin and asked him his advice in the matter.

They found him in the monastery garden, in the

company of the elder brothers, for the younger ones were detained by their work. He was digging up nettles and other weeds with a hoe, that the useful herbs might grow more vigorously. When they had explained to him the reason of their coming he sighed deeply, from the very bottom of his heart, and said in reply :—"If Charles thought my advice worth having he would not have treated me so harshly. I give him no advice. Go, tell him what you found me doing." They were afraid to go back to the dreaded emperor without a definite answer, and again and again asked him what message they should convey to their lord. Then at last he said in anger :—"I will send him no message except—what I am doing! I am digging up the useless growths in order that the valuable herbs may be able to develop more freely."

So they went away sorrowfully thinking that they were bringing back a foolish answer. When the emperor asked them upon their arrival what answer they were bringing, they answered sorrowfully that after all their labour and long journeying they could get no definite information at all. Then that most wise king asked them carefully where they had found Pippin, what he was doing, and what answer he had given them ; and they said : "We found him sitting on a rustic seat turning over the vegetable garden with a hoe. When we told him the cause of our journey we could extract no other reply than this, even by the greatest entreaties: 'I give no message, except—what I am doing! I am digging up the useless growths in order that the valuable herbs may be able to develop more freely.'" When he heard this the emperor, not lacking in cunning and mighty in wisdom, rubbed his ears and blew out his nostrils and said: "My good vassals, you have brought back a very reasonable answer." So while the messengers were fearing that they might be in peril of their lives, Charles was able to divine the real meaning of the words. He took all those plotters away from the land of the living; and so gave to his loyal subjects room to grow and spread, which had previously been occupied by those unprofitable servants. One of his enemies, who had chosen as his part of the spoil of the empire the highest hill in France and all that could be seen from it, was, by Charles's orders, hanged upon a high gallows on that very hill. But he bade his bastard son Pippin choose the manner of life that most pleased him. Upon this permission being given him, he chose a post in a monastery then most noble but now destroyed. (Who is there that does not know the manner of its destruction! But I will not tell the story of its fall until I see your little Bernard with a sword girt upon his thigh.)

The magnanimous Charles was often angry because he was urged to go out and fight against foreign nations, when one of his nobles might have accomplished the task. I can prove this from the action of one of my own neighbours. There was a man of Thurgau, of the name of Eishere, who as his name implies was "a great part of a terrible army" and so tall that you might have thought him sprung from the race of Anak, if they had not lived so long ago and so far away. Whenever he came to the river Dura and found it swollen and foaming with the torrents from the mountains, and could not force his huge charger to enter the stream (though stream I must not call it, but hardly melted ice), then he would seize the reins and force his horse to swim through behind him, saying: "Nay, by Saint Gall, you must come, whether you like it or not!"

Well, this man followed the emperor and mowed down the Bohemians and Wiltzes and Avars as a man might mow down hay; and spitted them on his spear like birds. When he came home the sluggards asked him how he had got on in the country of the Winides; and he, contemptuous of some and angry with others, replied: "Why should I have been bothered with those tadpoles? I used sometimes to spit seven or eight or nine of them on my spear and carry them about with me squealing in their gibberish. My lord king and I ought never to have been asked to weary ourselves in fighting against worms like those."

13. Now about the same time that the emperor was putting the finishing touch to the war with the Huns, and had received the surrender of the races that I have just mentioned, the Northmen left their homes and disquieted greatly the Gauls and the Franks. Then the unconquered Charles returned and tried to attack them by land in their own homes, by a march through difficult and unknown country. But, whether it was that the providence of God prevented it in order that, as the Scripture says, He might make trial of Israel, or whether it was that our sins stood in the way, all his efforts came to nothing. One night, to the serious discomfort of the whole army, it was calculated that fifty yoke of oxen belonging to one abbey had died of a sudden disease. Afterwards when Charles was making a prolonged journey through his vast empire, Gotefrid, king of the Northmen, encouraged by his absence, invaded the territory of the Frankish kingdom and chose the district of the Moselle for his home. But Gotefrid's

own son (whose mother he had just put away and taken to himself a new wife) caught him, while he was pulling off his hawk from a heron, and cut him through the middle with his sword. Then, as happened of old when Holofernes was slain, none of the Northmen dare trust any longer in his courage or his arms; but all sought safety in flight. And thus the Franks were freed without their own effort, that they might not after the fashion of Israel boast themselves against God. Then Charles, the unconquered and the invincible, glorified God for His judgment; but complained bitterly that any of the Northmen had escaped because of his absence. "Ah, woe is me!" he said, "that I was not thought worthy to see my Christian hands dabbling in the blood of those dog-headed fiends."

14. It happened too that on his wanderings Charles once came unexpectedly to a certain maritime city of Narbonensian Gaul. When he was dining quietly in the harbour of this town, it happened that some Norman scouts made a piratical raid. When the ships came in sight some thought them Jews, some African or British merchants, but the most wise Charles, by the build of the ships and their speed, knew them to be not merchants but enemies, and said to his companions: "These ships

are not filled with merchandise, but crowded with our fiercest enemies." When they heard this, in eager rivalry, they hurried in haste to the ships. But all was in vain, for when the Northmen heard that Charles, the Hammer, as they used to call him, was there, fearing lest their fleet should be beaten back or even smashed in pieces, they withdrew themselves, by a marvellously rapid flight, not only from the swords but even from the eyes of those who followed them. The most religious, just and devout Charles had risen from the table and was standing at an eastern window. For a long time he poured down tears beyond price, and none dared speak a word to him; but at last he explained his actions and his tears to his nobles in these words:—"Do you know why I weep so bitterly, my true servants? I have no fear of those worthless rascals doing any harm to me; but I am sad at heart to think that even during my lifetime they have dared to touch this shore; and I am torn by a great sorrow because I foresee what evil things they will do to my descendants and their subjects."

May the protection of our Master Christ prevent the accomplishment of this prophecy; may your sword, tempered already in the blood of the Nordostrani, resist it! The sword of your brother Carloman will help, which now lies idle and rusted, not for want of spirit, but for want of funds, and because of the narrowness of the lands of your most faithful servant Arnulf. If your might wills it, if your might orders it, it will easily be made bright and sharp again. These and the little shoot of Bernard form the only branch that is left of the once prolific root of Lewis, to flourish under the wonderful growth of your protection. Let me insert here therefore in the history of your namesake Charles an incident in the life of your great-great-grandfather Pippin: which perhaps some future little Charles or Lewis may read and imitate.

15. When the Lombards and other enemies of the Romans were attacking them, they sent ambassadors to this same Pippin, and asked him for the love of Saint Peter to condescend to come with all speed to their help. As soon as he had conquered his enemies he came victoriously to Rome, and this was the song of praise with which the citizens received him. "The fellow-citizens of the apostles and the servants of God have come to-day bringing peace, and making their native land glorious, to give peace to the heathen and to set free the people of the Lord." (Many people, ignorant of the meaning and origin of this song, have been accustomed to sing it on the birthdays of the apostles.) Pippin feared

the envy of the people of Rome (or, more truly, or Constantinople) and soon returned to Frankland.

When he found that the nobles of his army were accustomed in secret to speak contemptuously of him, he ordered one day a huge and ferocious bull to be brought out; and then a savage lion to be let loose upon him. The lion rushed with tremendous fury on the bull, seized him by the neck and cast him on the ground. Then the king said to those who stood round him: "Now, drag off the lion from the bull, or kill the one on the top of the other." They looked on one another, with a chill at their hearts, and could hardly utter these words amidst their sobs:—"Lord, what man is there under heaven, who dare attempt it?" Then Pippin rose confidently from his throne, drew his sword, and at one blow cut through the neck of the lion and severed the head of the bull from his shoulders. Then he put back his sword into its sheath and sat again upon his throne and said: "Well, do you think I am fit to be your lord? Have you not heard what the little David did to the giant Goliath, or what the child Alexander did to his nobles?" They fell to the ground, as though a thunderbolt had struck them, and cried: "Who but a madman would deny your right to rule over all mankind?"

Not only was his courage shown against beasts and men ; but he also fought an incredible contest against evil spirits. The hot baths at Aix had not yet been built ; but hot and healing waters bubbled from the ground. He ordered his chamberlain to see that the water was clean and that no unknown person was allowed to enter into them. This was done ; and the king took his sword and, dressed only in linen gown and slippers, hurried off to the bath ; when lo ! the Old Enemy met him, and attacked him as though he would slay him. But the king, strengthened with the sign of the cross, made bare his sword ; and, noticing a shape in human form, struck his unconquerable sword through it into the ground so far, that he could only drag it out again after a long struggle. But the shape was so far material that it defiled all those waters with blood and gore and horrid slime. But even this did not upset the unconquerable Pippin. He said to his chamberlain : "Do not mind this little affair. Let the defiled water run for a while ; and then, when it flows clear again, I will take my bath without delay."

16. I had intended, most noble emperor, to weave my little narrative only round your great-grandfather Charles, all of whose deeds you know

well. But since the occasion arose which made it necessary to mention your most glorious father Lewis, called the illustrious, and your most religious grandfather Lewis, called the pious, and your most warlike great-great-grandfather Pippin the younger, I thought it would be wrong to pass over their deeds in silence, for the sloth of modern writers has left them almost untold. There is no need to speak of the elder Pippin, for the most learned Bede in his ecclesiastical history has devoted nearly a whole volume to him. But now that I have recounted all these things by way of digression I must swim swan-like back to your illustrious namesake Charles. But, if I do not curtail somewhat his feats in war, I shall never come to consider his daily habits of life. Now I will give with all possible brevity the incidents that occur to me.

17. When after the death of the ever-victorious Pippin the Lombards were again attacking Rome, the unconquered Charles, though he was fully occupied with business to the north of the Alps, marched swiftly into Italy. He received the Lombards into his service after they had been humbled in a war that was almost bloodless, or (one might say), after they had surrendered of their own free will; and to prevent them from ever again revolting

from the Frankish kingdom or doing any injury to the territories of Saint Peter, he married the daughter of Desiderius, chief of the Lombards. But no long time afterwards, because she was an invalid and little likely to give issue to Charles, she was, by the counsel of the holiest of the clergy, put aside, even as though she were dead: whereupon her father in wrath bound his subjects to him by oath, and shutting himself up within the walls of Pavia, he prepared to give battle to the invincible Charles, who, when he had received certain news of the revolt, hurried to Italy with all speed.

Now it happened that some years before one of the first nobles, called Otker, had incurred the wrath of the most terrible emperor, and had fled for refuge to Desiderius. When the near approach of the dreaded Charles was known, these two went up into a very high tower, from which they could see anyone approaching at a very great distance. When therefore the baggage-waggons appeared, which moved more swiftly than those used by Darius or Julius, Desiderius said to Otker: "Is Charles in that vast army ?" And Otker answered: "Not yet." Then when he saw the vast force of the nations gathered together from all parts of his empire, he said with confidence to Otker: "Surely Charles moves in pride among those forces." But Otker answered: "Not yet, not yet." Then Desiderius fell into great alarm and said, "What shall we do if a yet greater force comes with him?" And Otker said, "You will see what he is like when he comes. What will happen to us I cannot say." And, behold, while they were thus talking, there came in sight Charles's personal attendants, who never rested from their labours; and Desiderius saw them and cried in amazement, "There is Charles." And Otker answered: "Not yet, not yet." Then they saw the bishops and the abbots and the clerks of his chapel with their attendants. When he saw them he hated the light and longed for death, and sobbed and stammered, "Let us go down to hide ourselves in the earth from the face of an enemy so terrible." And Otker answered trembling, for once, in happier days, he had had thorough and constant knowledge of the policy and preparations of the unconquerable Charles: "When you see an iron harvest bristling in the fields; and the Po and the Ticino pouring against the walls of the city like the waves of the sea, gleaming black with glint of iron, then know that Charles is at hand." Hardly were these words finished when there came from the west a black cloud, which turned the bright day to horrid gloom. But as the emperor drew nearer the gleam of the arms turned the darkness into day, a day darker than any night to that beleaguered garrison. Then could be seen the iron Charles, helmeted with an iron helmet, his hands clad in iron gauntlets, his iron breast and broad shoulders protected with an iron breast-plate: an iron spear was raised on high in his left hand; his right always rested on his unconquered iron falchion. The thighs, which with most men are uncovered that they may the more easily ride on horseback, were in his case clad with plates of iron: I need make no special mention of his greaves, for the greaves of all the army were of iron. His shield was all of iron: his charger was iron-coloured and iron-hearted. All who went before him, all who marched by his side, all who followed after him and the whole equipment of the army imitated him as closely as possible. The fields and open places were filled with iron; the rays of the sun were thrown back by the gleam of iron; a people harder than iron paid universal honour to the hardness of iron. The horror of the dungeon seemed less than the bright gleam of iron. "Oh the iron! Woe for the iron!" was the confused cry that rose from the citizens. The strong walls shook at the sight of the iron; the resolution of young and old fell before the iron. Now when the truthful Otker saw in one swift glance all this which

I, with stammering tongue and the voice of a child, have been clumsily explaining with rambling words, he said to Desiderius: "There is the Charles that you so much desired to see": and when he had said this he fell to the ground half dead.

But as the inhabitants of the city, either through madness or because they entertained some hope of resistance, refused to let Charles enter on that day, the most inventive emperor said to his men: "Let us build to-day some memorial, so that we may not be charged with passing the day in idleness. Let us make haste to build for ourselves a little house of prayer, where we may give due attention to the service of God, if they do not soon throw open the city to us." No sooner had he said it than his men flew off in every direction, collected lime and stones, wood and paint, and brought them to the skilled workmen who always accompanied him. And between the fourth hour of the day and the twelfth they built, with the help of the young nobles and the soldiers, such a cathedral, so provided with walls and roofs, with fretted ceilings and frescoes, that none who saw it could believe that it had taken less than a year to build. But, how on the next day some of the citizens wanted to throw open the gate; and some wanted to fight against him, even without hope of victory, or rather to fortify themselves against him; and how easily he conquered, took and occupied the city, without the shedding of blood, and merely by the exercise of skill;—all this I must leave others to tell, who follow your highness not for love, but in the hope of gain.

Then the most religious Charles marched on and came to the city of Friuli, which the pedants call Forum Julii. Now it happened just at this time that the bishop of that city (or, to use a modern word, the patriarch) was drawing near to the end of his life. Charles made haste to visit him, in order that he might designate his successor by name. But the bishop, with remarkable piety, sighed from the bottom of his heart and said: "Sire, I have held this bishopric for a long time without any use or profit; and now I leave it to the judgment of God and your disposal. For I do not wish, at the point of death, to add anything to the mountain of sin that I have heaped together during my life, for which I shall have to make answer to the inevitable and incorruptible Judge." The most wise Charles was so pleased with these words, that he rightly thought him the equal in virtue of the ancient fathers.

After Charles, of all the energetic Franks the most energetic, had stayed in that country for a short time, while he was appointing a worthy successor to the deceased bishop, one festal day after the celebration of mass he said to his retinue: "We must not let leisure lead us into slothful habits: let us go hunting and kill something; and let us all go in the very clothes that we are wearing at this moment." Now the day was cold and rainy and Charles was wearing a sheepskin, not much more costly than the cloak which Saint Martin wore when with bare arms he offered to God a sacrifice that received divine approval. But the others—for it was a holiday and they had just come from Pavia, whither the Venetians had carried all the wealth of the east from their territories beyond the sea—the others, I say, strutted in robes made of pheasant-skins and silk; or of the necks, backs and tails of peacocks in their first plumage. Some were decorated with purple and lemon-coloured ribbons; some were wrapped round with blankets and some in ermine robes. They scoured the thickets; they were torn by branches of trees, thorns, and briars; they were drenched with rain; they were defiled with the blood of wild beasts and the filth of the skins; and in this plight they returned home. Then the most crafty Charles said: "No one of us must take off his dress of skins before he goes to bed; they will dry better upon our bodies." Then everyone, more anxious about his body than his dress, made search for fire and tried to warm himself. Then they returned and remained in attendance upon Charles far into the night before they were dismissed to their apartments. Then when they began to draw off their dresses of skins and their slender belts, the creased and shrunken garments could be heard even from a distance cracking like sticks broken when they are dry: and the courtiers sighed and groaned and lamented that they had lost so much money on a single day. They had received however a command from the emperor to appear before him next day in the same skin-garments. When they came it was no longer the splendid show of yesterday; for they looked dirty and squalid in their discoloured and rent clothes. Then Charles, full of guile, said to his chamberlain: "Give my sheepskin a rub and bring it to me." It came quite white and perfectly sound and Charles took it and showed it to all those who were there and spoke as follows:—"Most foolish of mortal men! which of these dresses is the most valuable and the most useful, this one of mine which was bought for a piece of silver, or those of yours which you bought for pounds, nay for many talents?" Their eyes sank to the ground for they could not bear his most terrible censure.

Your most religious father imitated this example of the Great Charles all through his life, for he never allowed anyone, who seemed to him worthy of his notice or his teaching, to wear anything when on campaign against the enemy except the military accoutrements, and garments of wool and linen. If any of his servants, ignorant of this rule, happened to meet him with silk or silver or gold upon his person, he would receive a reprimand of the following kind and would depart a better and a wiser man. "Here's a blaze of gold and silver and scarlet! Why, you wretched fellow, can't you be satisfied with perishing yourself in battle if Fate so decides? Must you also give your wealth into the hands of the enemy; which might have gone to ransom your soul, but now will decorate the temples of the heathen?"

But now, though you know it better than I do, I will tell again how, from early youth up to his seventieth year, the unconquered Lewis delighted in iron; and what an exhibition of his fondness for iron he made in the presence of the legates of the Northmen!

18. When the kings of the Northmen sent gold and silver as witness of their loyalty and their swords as a mark of their perpetual subjection and surrender, the king gave orders that the precious metals should be

thrown upon the floor, and should be looked upon by all with contempt, and be trampled upon by all as though they were dirt. But, as he sat upon his lofty throne, he ordered the swords to be brought to him that he might make trial of them. Then the ambassadors, anxious to avoid the possibility of any suspicion of an evil design, took the swords by the very point (as servants hand knives to their masters) and thus gave them to the emperor at their own risk. He took one by the hilt and tried to bend the tip of the blade right back to the base; but the blade snapped between his hands which were stronger than the iron itself. Then one of the envoys drew his own sword from its sheath and offered it, like a servant, to the emperor's service, saying: "I think you will find this sword as flexible and as strong as your all-conquering right hand could desire." Then the emperor (a true emperor he! As the Prophet Isaiah says in his prophecy, "Consider the rock whence ye were hewn": for he out of all the vast population of Germany, by the singular favour of God, rose to the level of the strength and courage of an earlier generation)—the emperor, I say, bent it like a vine-twig from the extreme point back to the hilt, and then let it gradually straighten itself again. Then the envoys gazed upon one another and said in amazement:

"Would that our kings held gold and silver so cheap and iron so precious."

19. As I have mentioned the Northmen I will show by an incident drawn from the reign of your grandfather in what slight estimation they hold faith and baptism. Just as after the death of the warrior King David, the neighbouring peoples, whom his strong hand had subdued, for a long time paid their tribute to his peaceful son Solomon: even so the terrible race of the Northmen still loyally paid to Lewis the tribute which through terror they had paid to his father, the most august Emperor Charles. Once the most religious Emperor Lewis took pity on their envoys, and asked them if they would be willing to receive the Christian religion; and, when they answered that always and everywhere and in everything they were ready to obey him, he ordered them to be baptised in the name of Him, of whom the most learned Augustine says: "If there were no Trinity, the Truth would never have said: 'Go and teach all peoples, baptising them in the name of the Father, Son and Holy Ghost.'" The nobles of the palace adopted them almost as children, and each received from the emperor's chamber a white robe and from their sponsors a full Frankish attire, of costly robes and arms and other decorations.

This was often done and from year to year they came in increasing numbers, not for the sake of Christ but for earthly advantage. They made haste to come, not as envoys any longer but as loyal vassals, on Easter Eve to put themselves at the disposal of the emperor; and it happened that on a certain occasion they came to the number of fifty. The emperor asked them whether they wished to be baptised, and when they had confessed he bade them forthwith be sprinkled with holy water. As linen garments were not ready in sufficient numbers he ordered shirts to be cut up and sewn together into the fashion of wraps. One of these was forthwith clapped upon the shoulders of one of the elder men; and when he had looked all over it for a minute, he conceived fierce anger in his mind, and said to the emperor: "I have gone through this washing business here twenty times already, and I have been dressed in excellent clothes of perfect whiteness; but a sack like this is more fit for clodhoppers than for soldiers. If I were not afraid of my nakedness, for you have taken away my own clothes and have given me no new ones, I would soon leave your wrap and your Christ as well."

Ah! how little do the enemies of Christ value the words of the Apostle of Christ where he says:—"All ye that are baptised in Christ, put on Christ"; and again : "Ye that are baptised in Christ are baptised in His death" ; or that passage which is aimed especially at those who despise the faith and violate the sacraments : "Crucifying the Son of God afresh and putting Him to an open shame !" Oh ! would that this were the case only with the heathen ; and not also among those who are called by the name of Christ !

20. Now I must tell a story about the goodness of the first Lewis, and then I shall come back to Charles. That most peaceable emperor Lewis, being free from the incursions of the enemy, gave all his care to works of religion, as, for instance, to prayer, to works of charity, to the hearing and just determinations of trials at law. His talents and his experience had made him very skilful in this latter business ; and when one day there came to him one, who was considered a very Achitophel by all, and tried to deceive him he gave him this answer following, with courteous mien and kindly voice, though with some little agitation of mind. "Most wise Anselm," he said, "if I may be allowed to say so, I would venture to observe that you are deviating from the path of rectitude." From that day the reputation of that legal luminary sank to nothing in the eyes of all the world.

21. Moreover the most merciful Lewis was so intent on works of charity that he liked not merely to have them done in his sight, but even to do them with his own hand. Even when he was away he made special arrangements for the trial of cases in which the poor were concerned. He chose one of their own number, a man of small bodily strength, but apparently more courageous than the rest, and gave orders that he should decide offences committed by them; and should see to the restoration of stolen property, the requital of injuries and wounds, and in cases of greater crimes to the infliction of mutilation, decapitation, and the exposure of the bodies on the gallows. This man established dukes, tribunes, centurions and their representatives, and performed his task with energy.

Moreover the most merciful emperor, worshipping Christ in the persons of all the poor, was never weary of giving them food and clothing: and he did so especially on the day when Christ, having put off His mortal body, was preparing to take to Himself an incorruptible one. On that day it was his practice to make presents to each and every one of those who served in the palace or did duty in the royal court. He would order belts, leg coverings and precious garments brought from all parts of his vast empire to be given to some of his nobles; the lower orders would get Frisian cloaks of various colours; his grooms, cooks and kitchen-attendants got clothes of linen and wool and knives according to their needs. Then, when according to the Acts of the Apostles there was no one that was in need of anything, there was a universal feeling of gratitude. The ragged poor, now decently clad, raised their voices to heaven with the cry of "'Kyrie Eleison' to the blessed Lewis" through all the wide courts and the smaller openings of Aix (which the Latins usually call porches); and all the knights who could embraced the feet of the emperor; and those who could not get to him worshipped him afar off as he made his way to church. On one of these occasions one of the fools said in jest: "O happy Lewis, who on one day hast been able to clothe so many people. By Christ, I think that no one in Europe has clothed more than you this day except Atto." When the emperor asked him how it was possible that Atto should have clothed more, the jester, pleased to have secured the attention of the emperor, said with a grin: "He has distributed to-day a vast number of new clothes." The emperor, with the sweetest possible expression on his face, took this for the silly joke it was, and entered the church in humble devotion, and there behaved himself so reverently that he seemed to have our Lord Jesus Christ Himself before his bodily eyes.

It was his habit to go to the baths every Saturday, not for any need there was of it, but because it gave him an opportunity of making presents; for he used to give everything that he took off, except his sword and belt, to his attendants. His liberality reached even to the lowest grades: insomuch that he once ordered all his attire to be given to one Stracholf, a glazier, and a servant of Saint Gall. When the servants of the barons heard of this, they laid an ambuscade for him on the road and tried to rob him. Then he cried out: "What are you doing? You are using violence to the glazier of the emperor!" They answered: "You can keep your office but . . ."

[*Here the MS. ends, and the further adventures of Stracholf are left to conjecture.*]

NOTES

1, 1. Walafridus Strabo was abbot of a Frankish monastery from 842 to 849.

2, 20. The Emperor Lewis I. (Lewis the Pious, 814-840) was the son and successor of Charles the Great. His weakness and pietism did much to wreck the imperial structure of Charles.

3, 9. Neither the headings nor the decorations (incisiones) are given in the present translation. The decorations necessarily disappear, and the various headings to the paragraphs, not being the work of Eginhard, are not usually printed with the text. But Walafridus Strabo was personally known to Eginhard, and his Preface seems, therefore, to deserve reproduction.

5, 7. That is, though there are many who would be ready to write Charles's life, Eginhard thinks that he has peculiar qualifications for the task which make it obligatory on him to do so.

6, 17. The Latin of Eginhard's Life is much superior to the general monkish Latin of his period. *See* Introduction.

8, 3. This is King Childeric III., who was deposed in 751 by a National Council, with the approval of the Pope. Pippin the Short was then elected king, and crowned by Boniface. With Childeric the Merovingian dynasty ends, and gives place to the curiously-named Carolingian, of which Charlemagne was the greatest representative.

8, 4. Eginhard here makes a mistake. The Pope was not

Stephen, who held the Papal See from 752 to 757, but Zacharias, who was Pope from 741 to 752. Eginhard's mistake is, perhaps, due to the fact that the decision of Zacharias was confirmed by his successor.

9, 15. Mr Carless Davis remarks on this passage: "Eginhard errs in representing this as an indignity. Religious usage demanded that the king of the race should make his progresses in this primitive vehicle. The Merovingians were a national priesthood. Here also we have the explanation of their flowing locks and beard. The touch of steel—a metal unknown to the Frankish nation in its infancy—would have profaned their persons. Similarly the priesthood of ancient Rome were forbidden to remove the hair from their faces except with bronze tweezers." ("Life of Charlemagne," p. 28.)

9, 19. This is Charles Martel—Charles the Hammer—who "reigned" as Mayor of the Palace from 715 to 741. His great victory (variously known as the Battle of Poitiers, or the Battle of Tours, though the former is the more accurate title) was fought in 732, and is regarded as the "Salamis of Western Europe." It was the first serious blow that the Mohammedan advance had received, and its effects were decisive. The second battle, fought near Narbonne, completed the work of the first.

10, 1. Pippin, father of Charles Martel, and grandfather of Pippin the Short, was Mayor of the Palace from 687 to 714.

11, 7. Pippin's reign really lasted for rather more than sixteen years—from 751 to 768.

11, 20. This statement, as is clear from other sources, does not correspond with the facts. Charles took Austrasia, and the greater part of Neustria, with the lands lying between the Loire and the Garonne. Burgundy, Provence, Alsace, Alemannia, and the south-eastern part of Aquitaine fell to Carloman.

12, 9. Carloman died in December 771. His death removed from the path of Charles one of the most serious obstacles. The custom of the Frankish monarchy was equal inheritance of all the sons. It was this which contributed so much to the disruption of the Frankish power on the death of Charles; but for the death of Carloman the "Empire" would never have been founded, or founded only after bitter civil war. Eginhard again makes a mistake in dates. The two brothers had administered the realm in common for more than three years.

12, 11. This reticence of Eginhard's about his hero's early life, about which it would have been quite easy to procure information, has seemed to many to lend colour to a report that Charles was born before the Church had sanctioned the marriage of his parents.

13, 10. Hunold was the father of Waifar, and had for twenty years lived as a monk in the Island of Rhé, but upon the death of his son he left his monastic retreat in the hope of re-establishing the fortunes of his family in Aquitaine.

16, 3. The Saxon war—the greatest task of Charles's whole reign—lasted with some intermissions for more than thirty years (from 772 to 804). By his conquest and conversion of the fierce and heathen Saxons—who occupied the lands in the valleys of the Ems and the Weser and reached as far as the Elbe—he laid the foundations of mediæval and modern Germany.

16, 12. For an account of the religious beliefs and practices of the Saxons, *see* Davis's "Charlemagne," p. 95.

17, 10. The "conversion" of Saxony by Charles was of the most forcible kind. No Mohammedan ever offered the choice between the Koran and the edge of the sword more clearly than Charles put death or baptism before the Saxons. The "Saxon Poet," who in the next century wrote in honour of the King who had destroyed the independence of his land, tells how Charles used the whole force of his army to drag the Saxons from the devil's power; and remarks, as a matter of course, that persuasion and argument are not sufficient to turn the heathen from their faith.

18, 16. The river Hasa is near Osnabrück.

20, 20. This is the famous defeat of Roncesvalles, where later legends affirmed that "Charlemagne with all his peerage fell at Fontarabia," and where Roland wound his horn, whose sound is still heard in the verse of Milton. By a strange chance this incident becomes one of the most famous in the cycle of mediæval Charlemagne legends; and Roland, evermore transfigured from the historical warden of the Breton march, becomes, after long wanderings, the Orlando of the "Orlando Furioso" of Ariosto. But the historical Roland seems mentioned here, and here only.

21, 9. The Duchy of Beneventum embraced a large part of the Italian peninsula south of Rome. It had been for a long time connected, in loose feudal dependence, with the Lombard monarchy of North Italy, and, since that had been overwhelmed and annexed by Charles, was now regarded as a dependency of the Carolingian monarchy.

22, 3. Tassilo, Duke of Bavaria, had offended Charles by claiming independent sovereignty and refusing to recognise Charles in any way as his overlord. From the beginning of Charles's reign there had been friction between them, but for some time a hollow truce had existed. War came in 787, in spite of the efforts of the Papacy at mediation, and ended swiftly, as described in the text, owing to the overwhelming strength of the armies brought against Tassilo by Charles. But the past of Bavaria was too great to allow its Duke to accept the position of inferiority, and in the next year Tassilo was deposed, tonsured, and imprisoned in a monastery.

23, 3. It was part of Charles's general policy to displace the dukes of his realm, with their undefined and dangerous powers, and to administer his dominions by a large number of counts, who were to begin with quite dependent officials executing the orders of the King over a limited area. "Count" was not yet the great title of nobility which it became later.

23, 11. The Wiltzes lived on the shores of the Baltic between the Elbe and the Oder.

23, 14. This "gulf" of Eginhard's presents geographical difficulties. The direction indicated and the approximate measurements suggested make it impossible to apply his words to the whole of the Baltic Gulf. The south-eastern part of the Baltic will correspond fairly well to the description.

24, 3. The war against the Avars was due to the alliance which had existed between them and Tassilo, Duke of Bavaria. The Avars, though allied in race to the ancient Huns and the modern Magyars, were, nevertheless, a distinct people. Charles's war entirely broke their power, and removed a great danger from western Europe.

24. "The Monk of St Gall" (II. i.) gives an interesting description of the vast concentric earthworks by which the power of the Kagan was defended, and his account rests on better authority than much of his strange chronicle. *See* also Dr Hodgkin's "Life of Charles the Great," p. 155.

24, 12. The vast treasure of the Avars had an important influence on the course of Charles's career. This great influx of the precious metals into Germany depreciated the value of the coinage and raised the price of commodities.

25, 6. This is Tersatz, a town of Istria.

25, 22. These Northmen (or Danes, as they are usually called when they appear in English history) proved themselves the most terrible enemies of civilisation during the next century. "The Monk of St Gall" makes Charles prophesy the ruin that would come eventually on his Empire from these northern sea-rovers. The attacks of the Northmen were among the most direct causes of the subsequent disruption of the Empire of Charles.

26, 20. This is an exaggeration of Eginhard's. Charles did, indeed, greatly extend the Frankish dominions; but he strengthened them still more decisively by the improvements which he introduced into the internal order and administration.

26, 23. The Balearic Sea is the western Mediterranean.

28, 10. "Non aliter quam proprium suum." Feudalism in any strict sense of the word was not yet established; but Alfonso was, in effect, "commending" himself to a feudal superior.

28, 16. The spelling of the original is retained; but the "Aaron" of Eginhard is the great Caliph Harun-al-Raschid, the Abassid Caliph of Bagdad, whose actions play so large a part in fiction as well as in history.

29, 4. It is strange, in view of the friendly relations of Charles with the Mohammedan ruler of the East, that later legend so persistently represented Charles as a Crusader, driving the Paynim from the Holy City. The height of unreality is reached when, as in Ariosto, we find Charlemagne relieving the city of Paris, which is being besieged by the Mohammedans.

29, 9. This elephant caused a great sensation in Europe. His arrival, life, and death are carefully noted by the chroniclers.

29, 26. The exact meaning of the original is far from clear (ne qua hostis exire potuisset). The ingress rather than the egress is what Charles must have wished to prevent, but there seems no doubt about the reading.

32, 12. "The Monk of St Gall" says that the cause of this repudiation was the constant illness of his wife, and her incapacity to bear him children.

32, 14. This Hildigard was only thirteen years of age at the time of her marriage with Charles. Besides the children mentioned by Eginhard she bore to Charles three others—Lothaire, Adelais, and Hildigard.

33, 4. Fastrada is regarded by Eginhard elsewhere as the evil influence on Charles's life, urging him against the natural bent of his character to acts of cruelty and violence. Dr Hodgkin, however, points out that the most cruel act of his reign—the massacre of 4500 Saxons—took place before his marriage with Fastrada.

34, 17. The betrothal of Hruotrud to the Eastern Emperor, and the rupture of the marriage contract, is a somewhat obscure thread in the diplomacy of the reign of Charles. Note that the betrothal took place in 781, during the residence of Charles at Rome, but nineteen years before he had assumed the imperial title. Religious difference and political jealousies probably both played their part in the rupture.

Both Frankish and Greek chroniclers are anxious to maintain that the repudiation came from their side.

36, 1. If scandal is to be believed, the Court of Charles, in spite of his devotion to the Church and his anxiety to maintain a high standard of morals, was the scene of much licence and disorder.

36, 5. This conspiracy of Pippin took place in the years 785 and 786.

40, 17. We have here the natural and simple beginnings of the ceremony that afterwards reached such great proportions in the *lever* and *coucher* of the French kings.

41, 5. This reference to Greek at the Court of Charlemagne is interesting in view of the exaggerated views sometimes held on the disappearance of Greek in the Middle Ages.

41, 14. This is Alcuin of York, one of the greatest of Englishmen, undoubtedly, as Eginhard says, the most learned man of his time. His letters form a valuable source of information for the inner life of Charlemagne and his Court.

41, 21. This passage has been closely scrutinised and commented on. Do Eginhard's words imply that Charlemagne could not write at all? This seems a very improbable interpretation of them. *Parum successit* would rather mean that "he made but little headway." It may well be that the King was able to write roughly and in an ordinary way but failed to acquire the elegant and delicate caligraphy that was aimed at by the scribes of the time

44, 8. Eginhard passes very lightly over these epoch-making events of Christmas Day in the year 800, when the imperial title was again assumed by a ruler of the West, and the Mediæval Empire was launched with all its vast consequences, both for the theory and practice of the Middle Ages.

Charlemagne's expressed regret for what occurred (of which we hear from other sources) has been variously interpreted. It can hardly refer to the imperial title altogether; for this certainly was not unexpected, nor was it due merely to the decision of the Pope. Charles had himself decided to adopt it: it was the coping-stone to all his policy and his whole career, for in power Charles was Emperor before the consecration of that famous Christmas Day. The regret expressed by Charles more probably refers to the method in which the title was bestowed: it came to him too much as a grant from the Papacy, too little as the result of his own power and will. His heart may well have foreboded something of the long struggle between Empire and Papacy, which agitated the eleventh, twelfth, and thirteenth centuries, which caused so much bloodshed on both sides of the Alps, and which in the end ruined the power of both Emperor and Pope: for this struggle had its roots in the indefinite basis of the imperial title. The regrets of Charlemagne are probably in close relation to the wars of Henry IV., of Frederick Barbarossa, and of Frederick II. Had the Papacy the right to give or to withhold the imperial title? That was the great underlying problem of the imperial position.

44, 14. The Roman Emperors are the Emperors at Constantinople.

44, 20. That is to say, the legal systems of the Salian and Ripuarian Franks.

45, 4. Nothing in all the policy of Charles gives such an impression of enlightenment as the actions alluded to here. A collection of German sagas, and a grammar of the German language as it was in the year 800—what would not posterity give for these? The disappearance of the former is due to the policy of his son and successor Lewis the Pious, whose piety had little in common with the robust and broad views of his father. The biographer of Lewis tells us that Lewis "rejected the national poems, which he had learnt in his youth, and would not have them read or recited or taught."

45. 8, Their names (in the original) are as follows:—Wintarmanoth, Hornung, Lentzinmanoth, Ostarmanoth, Winnemanoth, Brachmanoth, Hewimanoth, Aranmanoth, Witumanoth, Windumemanoth, Herbistmanoth, Heiligmanoth.

47, 22. This curt and definite statement of Eginhard disposes at once of the well-known story of Otto III.'s visit to Charlemagne's grave in the year 1000, and his remarkable discovery there. But the story is so famous that it may be given in the words of the chronicler of Novalese, who is our chief authority for it.

"After the passage of many years the Emperor Otto III. came into the district where the body of Charles was lying duly buried. He descended into the place of burial with two bishops and Otto, Count of Lomello; the Emperor himself completed the party of four. Now, the Count gave his version of what happened much as follows:—'We came then to Charles. He was not lying down, as is usual with the bodies of the dead, but sat on a sort of seat, as though he were alive. He was crowned with a golden crown; he held his sceptre in his hands, and his hands were covered with gloves, through which his nails had forced a passage. Round him there was a sort of vault built, strongly made of mortar and marble. When we came to the grave we broke a hole into it and entered, and entering, were aware of a very strong odour. At once we fell upon our knees and worshipped him, and the Emperor Otto clothed him with white garments, cut his nails, and restored whatever was lacking in him. But corruption had not yet taken anything away from his limbs; only a little was lacking to the very tip of his nose. Otto had this restored in gold; he then took a single tooth from his mouth, and so built up the vault, and departed.'"

59, 3. The reference is to the Book of Daniel ii. 33.

60, 26. The pilgrimage is, of course, life.

61, 12. The visit of Albinus (or Alcuin) of York to the court of King Charles is alluded to in Eginhard's Life of Charles, Ch. xxv. His arrival in Frankland occurred in 781, and was of the utmost importance in stimulating and guiding the intellectual renascence of Charles's reign.

66, 20. "Lord, if I am still useful to thy people I will willingly take on myself this labour on their behalf. Thy will be done" is the full versicle, which comes on the 11th November (St Martin's Day). The story in the text is made intelligible when we find that more than one of the responses that follow end with the words "Thy will be done." The poor clerk knew that, and started off, therefore, on the Lord's Prayer, which he knew would bring him to the right ending.

71, 7. Grimald was Abbot of St Gall from 841 to 872. It will be noticed all through the piece that the narrative becomes more full and definite, though not necessarily more truthful, when it touches on the writer's own monastery.

72, 22. The whole of this statement is a tissue of absurdities, which are, however, worth a moment's attention, as giving some indication of the value that is to be attached to the Monk of St Gall's testimony. The Pope Stephen here alluded to must be Stephen II., who occupied the Papal throne from 752 to 757. He it was who crowned Pippin King of the Franks in 754. He can have had nothing to do with Charlemagne, who did not reign until 768; but the words of the text (*se ad gubernacula regni perunxit*) can only refer to Charles. It must have been Pope Stephen III. (768-772) to whom Charlemagne appealed if there is any truth in the story at all; and Pope Stephen III. can, of course, have had nothing to do with Hilderich.

74, 13. Pope Leo III. did not succeed Pope Stephen until after an interval of twenty-three years. Pope Leo III.'s date is 795-816.

75, 2. For Drogo *see* Eginhard's Life, Ch. xv. But again the unhistorical character of the narrative is shown by the fact that Drogo was made Bishop of Metz, *after the death of Charles*, and against his own will.

75, 9. A curious display of trivial learning! But it is interesting to note the mention of Greek as of a language not wholly unknown to a monk of the ninth century.

75, 22. *See* Eginhard's Life, Ch. xxiv., for the difficulties found by Charles in observing the fasts of Lent.

82, 21. Here is another notorious error. Hildigard died in 783. Fastrada was queen when, in 791, Charles advanced to the war against the Avars.

88, 6. The next six chapters are omitted, because in them the Monk of St Gall is led away, by his desire to tell a good and edifying story, into matter that has no connection of any kind with Charlemagne, and is sometimes offensive to modern taste. The stories are for the most part to the discredit of the Episcopal order. A single phrase in Chapter xxv. may be noted, as indicating the theocratic view of Charles which the writer takes throughout: "the most religious Charles" is called *episcopus episcoporum*, "the bishop of bishops."

88, 22. Our author here again handles events of the most general notoriety in a spirit completely independent of historical accuracy. Leo III. was, it is true, the Pope to whose assistance Charlemagne came; but no Michael was ruling at that time in Constantinople. Michael II. reigned from 820-829, and Michael III. from 842-867. Thus the name was associated, in the mind of the Monk of St Gall, with the imperial throne of the east—and that was more than enough. The sentiment attributed to the Emperor is as impossible as his name is inaccurate.

90, 14. St Pancras is one of the saints given by the persecution of the Emperor Diocletian to the calendar of the Church He is said to have been executed in his fourteenth year in the year 295. The following extract from the Golden Legend will explain the reference in the text:—

"Of him said Gregory of Tours, Doctor: That if there be a man that will make a false oath in the place of his sepulchre, tofore or he came to the chancel of the quire he shall be travailed with an evil spirit and out of mind, or he shall fall on the pavement all dead. It happed on a time that there was a great altercation between two men, and the judge wist not who had wrong. And, for the jealousy of justice that he had, he brought them both unto the altar of Saint Peter for to swear, praying the apostle that he would declare who had right. And when he that had wrong had sworn and had none harm the judge who knew the malice of him said all on high: This old Peter here is either over-merciful, or he is propitious to this young man, but let us go to Pancrace and demand we of him the truth; and when they came to the sepulchre, he that was culpable swore and stretched forth his hand, but he might not withdraw his hand again to him, and anon after he died there, and therefore unto this day, of much people it is used that for great and notable causes men make their oaths upon the relics of S. Pancrace."

91, 4. This celebrated coronation took place on Christmas Day of the year 800, and marks the foundation of the Mediæval Empire. Charles is known to have expressed regret either at the fact or the manner of the presentation of the imperial crown; and the Monk of St Gall is not so wide of the point as usual in the account he gives of the causes of his hesitation.

98, 14. Giants figure largely in the stories which are told of St Antony's temptation. The Golden Legend says: "S. Anthony recordeth of himself that he had seen a man so great and so high that he vaunted himself to be the virtue and the providence of God and said to me: 'Demand of me what thou wilt, and I shall give it to thee.' And I spit in the midst of his visage, and anon I armed me with the sign of the cross, and ran upon him, and anon he vanished away. And after this the devil appeared to him in so great stature that he touched the heaven, etc." Gigantic appearances figure, too, elsewhere in the story of St Antony's trials.

100, 3. Two motives are to be detected in most of these stories beyond the general purpose of moral and religious edification. There is the jealousy of the bishops, so usually felt by the monks, and there is the scorn felt by the northern peoples for the refinements of the Italian population.

101, 13. I have inserted the passage in brackets, which seems necessary to give meaning to the following instances.

103, 19. This King of the Franks is, of course, not Charlemagne, but Charles the Third, called the Fat, who in 883 spent three days in the Monastery of St Gall.

105, 5. Julian's death took place in 367. It need scarcely be pointed out that the Monk's historical narrative is here of the very wildest description.

105, 15. It is unnecessary to disentangle the Monk's strange perversion of history; but it may be noted that he identifies the Avars, whom Charlemagne subdued, with the Huns who followed Attila. But the Huns and the Avars, though allied in race, were two quite distinct nationalities.

106, 9. It would be an interesting inquiry whether archæological or historical research corroborates in any way this interesting account which Adalbert gives of the Hunnish fortifications.

114, 12. These three sons are—Charles, who died in 811; Pippin, who died in 810; and Lewis, who succeeded to the undivided dominions of Charlemagne, and is usually known as Lewis the Pious.

117, 11. The Persians of the ninth century are by the Monk identified with the Persians of the period of Marathon and Salamis.

119, 13. It must be remembered that the whole of the Monk's narrative is nominally addressed to Charles the Fat, great-grandson of Charlemagne.

121, 4. This is the famous Haroun al Raschid already mentioned in Eginhard's Life of Charlemagne.

124, 18. There is really no doubt about the identification of the Arar. It is the Saône, the most important of the tributaries of the Rhone.

125, 7. This is Lewis of Bavaria, who was King of Germany from 843-876, the son of Lewis the Pious, and the father of Charles the Fat.

126, 20. The Monk's method here is not difficult to understand. The words of St Ambrose and the parallel between the Saint and Charles are clearly introduced to give evidence of the writer's wide learning.

128, 21. Charles the Fat had no children; but he had a brother, Carloman, King of Bavaria, and another, Lewis, King of Saxony.

129, 11. St Hemmeramm (or Emmeran, as the name is

now usually written) was first a bishop in some Frankish see (possibly Poitiers) who about 649 went as a missionary to the idolaters of Bavaria. He was assassinated in 652 near Munich, on his road to Rome. A church in Regensburg is still called by his name.

131, 25. This conspiracy is given in Eginhard's Life, Chap. xx., but without the Monk's picturesque details, and with the substitution of Prumia (in the Moselle country) for the Monastery of St Gall. Eginhard's authority must, of course, be preferred, and we have, therefore, a striking instance of the monkish chronicler's desire to turn everything to the honour of his own cloister.

134. 2. This story has a long history. It is first told of Thrasybulus, tyrant of Miletus; it was then adapted by Livy (1-54) to Tarquin, King of Rome, with slight alterations. The same story, which is here told somewhat clumsily, and applied to Charlemagne, is given by Ekkehard as belonging to the reign of Charles III.

135, 25. The reference is to the Monastery of Prumia, which was destroyed by the Northmen in 882.

136, 8. Thurgau is in Switzerland.

136, 9. "Eis," meaning terrible; and "here" an army.

137, 25. No Northman made any permanent settlement on the Moselle either in the reign of Charles or at any other time. At most this can refer only to the boast, or design, of some such chief as Gotefrid.

140, 3. The allusion to the Nordostrani fixes this reference to the year 882, when the Northmen were a terrible and increasing danger to all Frankland The Arnulf here mentioned was the son of Charles the Fat, and, later, Emperor.

140, 18. This story of King Pippin's visit to Rome is entirely legendary. It is repeated by later chroniclers, but is certainly without basis of any kind.

157, 19. I confess myself unable to make anything out of the jester's references to Atto.

INDEX

Printed at THE BALLANTYNE PRESS
SPOTTISWOODE, BALLANTYNE & CO. LTD.
Colchester, London & Eton, England

CPSIA information can be obtained at www.ICGtesting.com
Printed in the USA
BVOW09s1546040716

454354BV00024B/288/P